The Thinking Child Resource Book

If you are planning for a year, sow rice;
if you are planning for a decade, plant trees;
if you are planning for a lifetime,
educate people.

Chinese proverb

The Thinking Child Resource Book

Nicola Call

with Sally Featherstone

Published by Network Educational Press Ltd
PO Box 635
Stafford
ST16 1BF

First published 2003
© Nicola Call 2003

ISBN 1 85539 161 9

Project manager: Martha Harrison
Design & layout: Neil Hawkins, NEP
Illustrations: Kerry Ingham
Front cover illustration: Kerry Ingham

Printed in Great Britain by
MPG Books Ltd, Bodmin, Cornwall

Preface

This book is intended to be used as a companion to *The Thinking Child – Brain-based learning for the foundation stage*. In *The Thinking Child*, you will find the theory about brain-based learning and descriptions of the research that backs up the methods and practices described in both books. It is important to have an overview of this theory in order to have maximum success in putting these brain-based techniques into practice. It would therefore be preferable to read *The Thinking Child* before moving on to use the suggestions in this book.

Once you are familiar with *The Thinking Child*, you will see that the structure of *The Thinking Child Resource Book* is very much the same. This book is also divided into an introduction and then four parts, which are subdivided into section steps. In order to help you to use both books in tandem, cross references are given to *The Thinking Child* in the margin. These cross references provide the background theory for the practical suggestions given in this book. If there is a possibility that an activity or suggestion taken out of context may be inappropriate for use with some children or settings, a warning is given through a caution sign.

In this book, the main aspects of brain-based learning are given context through either a case study, where we describe real children in real settings, or an anecdote about one of 'Our four children'. These four pre-schoolers, who were described in detail in *The Thinking Child*, are George, Carrie, Kishan and Samantha. They are fictitious characters from settings that use brain-based learning techniques, and the descriptions of their activities are representative of some of the best early years practice.

Some of the resources in this book are intended for photocopying for use while working with children, for staff development or for individual reference. Many suggestions are given in the form of lists which can be easily photocopied, such as ways to help children develop high self-esteem, ways to give positive feedback or ways to involve parents in your setting. These suggestions can be used as described or can be developed to suit your individual situation. Other sections give practical activities to do with children, such as circle time activities and games to promote a 'can do' attitude. At various points, you will find a suggestion for a practical task, called 'Activity', that you may wish to undertake either alone or with colleagues. Again, these can be adapted to suit each individual setting. Material that is printed within the text in a small version on a clipboard, can be found in a full-sized version for photocopying at the end of the book.

Working to understand how the child's brain develops and applying this knowledge to early years practice is no small undertaking. The challenge may be great but the rewards of working this way are immeasurable. We sincerely hope that *The Thinking Child* and *The Thinking Child Resource Book* will help you as you make that learning journey.

gives cross reference to the topic in *The Thinking Child*.

 describes aspects of brain-based learning in real settings.

 describes aspects of brain-based learning in a fictitious setting of one of 'Our four children'.

 represents a small copy of the A4 size poster, which can be found in the Appendices starting on page 141.

 gives warning that activities taken out of context may be inappropriate for use with some children or settings.

Acknowledgements

Thank you to the many practitioners who generously shared their ideas and creativity with me. Working with Sally Featherstone has once again been both a pleasure and a great learning experience for me. Thanks are due to Sharon James, Heather Anderson, Jill Koops, Kate Barnes and Siobhan Burrows for their continued input and inspiration. The staff and children from Seer Green Church of England Combined School and Braunstone Frith Infant School welcomed us into their classrooms to do our research for this book.

Above all, thank you to my husband, Josef, for providing the encouragement and practical support that enables me to continue to write while being a mother. Thank you to Sara Arola for giving such excellent care to my own pre-schooler, Alysia, as I worked to meet my deadline, and to my baby, Rebecca, for snuggling so happily in her sling each morning as I worked. My children are my inspiration and my greatest teachers. I thank them for sharing with me the joys of the early years.

Contents

Understanding the child's brain

Step 1: About brain-based learning

In recent years researchers have begun to understand more about the brain, and the mysteries of intelligence have begun to unravel. Scientists are now able to look deep inside the living, functioning brain, and many long-held theories are being disproved and new ones developed.

Brain page 10

The brain consists of about one hundred billion nerve cells, called *neurons*. These neurons develop *dendrites* for transmitting information to other neurons and *axons* for receiving information. As patterns of thought are repeated, the participating neurons build stronger and more direct pathways, which are called *synapses*. The first few years of life in fact are the most critical for this wiring of the brain, and the more stimulation a child's brain receives, the more neural pathways are formed. As he repeats experiences, this pathway-building becomes permanent and strong – in other words, the experiences are committed to memory. In this way, nature and nurture act together to wire each individual child's brain in its own unique way. We cannot alter nature, but as practitioners we can provide the nurturing environment that will maximize the child's brain development.

When we use brain-based learning techniques, we are adapting the learning environment to take account of what scientists have found to be the best ways to help children to form these neural connections. That is what this book is about: applying current knowledge about the brain to the early years setting. Developing brain-based learning techniques can be exciting and extremely rewarding. We hope that this book and *The Thinking Child* will help you to put these techniques into practice with confidence.

Fascinating Facts

- Until very recently, it was thought that the functions of the various areas of the brain were pre-programmed and that damage to one area of the brain caused, for example, by a stroke, was irreparable. The latest research, however, has shown that the brain exhibits some level of structural *plasticity*. In other words, completely new wiring can actually be created, and some areas of the brain can take on entirely new roles after physical damage has occurred to other sections.

- Nutrition directly affects IQ. In 1988 a group of researchers from Christchurch School of Medicine in New Zealand followed more than 1,000 children from birth to age 18 to study the effects of breastfeeding.[1] They found a direct correlation between the higher scores in tests of cognitive ability and the duration of breastfeeding. Other studies have shown the seriousness of iron deficiency on the developing brain. Iron is needed for *myelination*, the process by which the axons are coated with a greasy substance called myelin. Without adequate myelin, the communication between brain cells becomes sluggish. Iron deficiency in young children can lead to poor cognitive development.[2]

- Language is linked to the ability to lay down memories. A team of researchers from New Zealand conducted a study to discover why most people do not have memories from before the age of three or four years. They played a specific game with children on two separate occasions. Most children were able to describe the game at the second visit, yet even when a child knew a word at the later date, he did not use it if it had not been in his vocabulary at the first visit.[3]

Step 2: Meeting the children in their settings

The setting

Our setting is a fictitious one that is designed to give an overview of what can be achieved when practitioners use brain-based learning techniques. The setting consists of a part-time pre-school situated in the church hall, which is just across the playground from the primary school, and a nursery and reception class within the school. The practitioners here enjoy a strong relationship and work to ensure that there is good continuity and progression between the three groups. They have been using brain-based techniques for several years and are continually evaluating their work and developing new ideas in line with the most recent research into the brain and child development.

Our four children are George, who attends the pre-school; Carrie, who attends the morning nursery; and Kishan and Samantha, who are both in the full-time reception class. These children are not 'case studies'. They are fictitious characters who illustrate how learning is affected by the choices made by adults around them. They are all fortunate enough to come from homes where their physical, intellectual and emotional needs are well met, yet they each have their own unique learning style. The practitioners work hard to try to match the curriculum to the wide variety of learners in their settings.

The children

Let's meet George

George is the one of the youngest children in the pre-school, which he attends three mornings per week. He is the only child in his family and receives considerable attention from his extended family. He is a quiet, gentle and tactile child, who is somewhat wary of new situations and often wants to follow the lead of other children.

George can be easily discouraged and frequently needs adult support when he encounters a challenge. Like many very young children, he tends to leave a task if he does not experience immediate success. His key-worker also feels that he needs to learn to become more assertive in group situations. He is now developing a few strong friendships with children in his group and is starting to engage in associative play more frequently. One of George's favourite activities is to work in the garden, watering plants, digging, weeding and observing nature. He notices details about the natural world and is one of the first to see any change in the outdoor environment, such as a plant flowering or a new weed growing through a crack in the pavement. Using Howard Gardner's definitions of the 'multiple intelligences',[4] George can be seen to have a strong naturalist intelligence.

Multiple intelligence page 122

Let's meet Carrie

Carrie is the oldest child in the morning group of the nursery class. Her mother is a single parent who has to commute several miles to work. Carrie goes to a breakfast club before school and is cared for by a local childminder in the afternoons and during school holidays. One of Carrie's greatest strengths is her interpersonal and intrapersonal skills. She relates well to other children and adults, and talks comfortably about how she feels. She is sensitive to the feelings of other children and loves to organize other children and look after them if they are hurt or unhappy.

Carrie is naturally a strong visual learner who can re-create a game with the small world toys, for example, from memory. She likes to get involved with very elaborate imaginative play involving other children, but she sometimes finds it difficult to settle for a sustained period, becoming distracted by the excitement of her stream of new ideas. Carrie needs help to maintain her focus and follow an activity through to its conclusion.

Let's meet Kishan

Kishan has been in reception class for two terms. He didn't attend either the pre-school or the nursery class previously, because he was settled at the full-time day-care centre that he attended from the age of three months. Kishan's family is bilingual. His parents are the first generation of their families to be born in the United Kingdom, and speak Bengali and English fluently.

Kishan has a highly inquisitive nature combined with boundless energy. He is a kinesthetic learner who also has a strong mathematical-logical intelligence. He has strengths in activities that involve spatial awareness. He needs to move in order to internalize information and he is always on the go. Consequently, Kishan sometimes needs help with his friendships. He finds it difficult to think through an action in preparation for an event. This can lead him into conflict with his peers. He needs to be allowed plenty of time to process information and benefits from being given explicit instructions and feedback about his behaviour.

Let's meet Samantha

Samantha also attends the full-time reception class. She has a strong linguistic intelligence and was a particularly early talker. By her first birthday she had a vocabulary of about 30 words, and from that point onwards her language acquisition was explosive. She enjoys story-telling sessions and does not need pictures as an aid to concentration. Her mother noticed that Samantha pole-bridged instinctively as a toddler, and she still finds it easy to talk her way through an activity now. She listens well, and finds it relatively easy to follow what her teacher is writing or drawing on the whiteboard as she gives an explanation to the group.

Pole-bridging page 86

Samantha also has a strong musical intelligence. She has a good sense of rhythm and pitch, and can recall a simple pattern and tune after hearing it just once. She finds it easy to learn while music is playing and is often the first child to recognize a CD when her teacher uses it to give a cue that a session is about to begin or come to an end. Samantha likes to stay indoors to read, draw or play in the home corner, and needs encouragement to join activities out of doors.

Preparing the climate and context for learning

Step 1: Addressing children's physical needs

Abraham Maslow's 'hierarchy of needs'[5] gives a good overview of the physical needs that must be met if children are to learn effectively. They can be thought of as a pyramid, with each of these needs being a layer upon which the next can be laid. The physiological needs are the basis of the pyramid. They can be broken down into five areas: hydration, nutrition, sleep, movement and attentional systems. It is the practitioner's responsibility to ensure that to the best of her ability she provides for these hierarchical needs and educates children about their importance. Here are some suggestions of some practical ways to do this.

Hierarchy of needs
page 29

Hydration

A reception class teacher shared with us her experience of introducing sports bottles in the classroom:

We decided as a school policy to address the issue of physiology and learning. As a part of this strategy we asked parents to provide their children with a water bottle that could be kept in the classroom so that children could drink freely.

The children were so excited the first day when they came into school clutching their bottles, that they wouldn't stay in their places for more than two minutes before going for a drink. I was tempted to set limits, but decided to just wait and see if the novelty wore off. Within two days, the trips to the bottles (and the loo!) became significantly less disruptive, and within a week children were only going to the refreshment table when they were really thirsty. It showed me that if you trust children, they will respond. If I hadn't trusted them, I would only have swapped one unsatisfactory system for another.

In one nursery, the adults and children had easy access to water, but when they were busy, they forgot to take a drink. The adults discussed this with the children and introduced a reminder signal. Now whenever an adult or child remembers to have a drink of water, they pick up the rain stick near the water table and turn it. Everyone stops at this sound to decide whether or not they are thirsty (most decide they are!). They then take a drink if they need it.

To ensure that children do not become dehydrated, you could:

- Build in regular social times for drinks and snacks throughout the day.
- Allow adequate time for children to have drinks at the end of sessions and during breaks.
- Encourage children to use refillable sports-style water bottles with sealable nozzles.
- Provide jugs of water and cups for the children to help themselves.
- Build in times when children can have a drink between activities.
- Talk about the importance of drinking enough water.
- Role-model by drinking water throughout the day yourself.
- Make sure children have access to water outside as well as inside, particularly on hot days. A small table or tray of bottles will remind them.
- Give regular reminders about drinking water, particularly during the first few weeks.

Encourage children to use sports-style water bottles.

Nutrition

A child's comment alerted a nursery teacher to poor messages often given in our culture about diet:

I was reading a story to a group of children about the day-to-day activities of a baby. It was a book by a well-known and respected publisher. I was reading on 'auto-pilot' when a child suddenly commented 'Oooh, yummy, a delicious cookie!' The text actually read 'I can taste a delicious cookie.' Why not 'a delicious apple' or 'a delicious banana'? We used that book as a starting point for discussion about delicious foods, but I then became much more conscious of the messages that we were giving children, not only through books but also through general conversation about food.

The practitioner arranged an audit of the books in her book corner and removed some of the books that gave poor messages about food. She made a conscious effort to select books with more positive messages in the future.

In one innovative nursery school, every other Wednesday was community lunch day. The children spent the morning preparing and cooking a lunch that they would eat together at midday. Often the meal would have a theme, and all the cultures of the class were represented. Parents came into school to help to make the meal with the children and shared in the preparation of healthy menus. Music was played through these special mealtimes, and time was taken to eat at leisure and to learn from the experience. On one occasion all the children made valiant efforts to eat an entire Chinese meal with chopsticks, and on another, they carefully unfolded pasta as it emerged from a pasta machine.

Children can help to prepare healthy snacks.

Fascinating Fact

A government initiative, the 'National School Fruit Scheme', is now underway.[6] Research shows that good nutrition leads to better learning. If all school children aged between four and six were to eat their allocated piece of free fruit each day, not only would the government be investing in better health, but also in better brains for the future.

To help children who may not have a nutritional diet, you could:

- Introduce a breakfast club.
- Provide healthy mid-morning and mid-afternoon snacks.
- Involve the children in preparing snacks and drinks.
- Encourage children to bring fruit or other healthy snacks to school for breaks.
- Introduce community lunch days on a weekly, monthly or half-termly basis.
- Educate children about nutrition and healthy eating.
- Read books and tell stories with positive messages about good nutrition.
- Monitor the subliminal messages given out about food through conversation or stories.
- Monitor lunch boxes and check what is eaten.
- Provide healthy pretend food for role play activities.
- Ensure that cooking activities include making healthy foods.
- Grow foods from packs of seeds, such as cress, tomatoes, beans, bean sprouts or lettuce.
- Plant seeds from fruit and vegetables to encourage interest in how plants grow, such as carrot tops, apple pips and avocado stones.
- Join the 'National Fruit Scheme'.

Sleep

One reception teacher suggested an activity for children to do at home where they each kept a sleep diary. She encouraged children to borrow books from the book corner to read at bedtime as they snuggled with their parents to go to sleep. Displays in the classroom showed the wonderful, pleasant aspects of bedtime: stories, cuddles, warm sheets, soft toys, music and togetherness.

When Carrie first started in the nursery, her mother began to have problems getting her to sleep at a reasonable time at night. Her mother spoke to the teacher. The teacher was pleased to get the chance to discuss this, as she had noticed that Carrie was often tired and not in the best mood for learning. She wondered if this could simply be an adjustment period for Carrie as she got accustomed to being in nursery five mornings per week.

They discussed Carrie's bedtime routine. Because her mother had a long commute from work, it was late before she collected Carrie from her childminder's house. This meant that their bedtime routine started late in the evening. Carrie's teacher suggested that her childminder could be asked to create a quiet time 15 minutes before her mother arrived. When Carrie's mother talked to the childminder, they also agreed that she would have Carrie's belongings organized at the door so that they could leave more quickly and quietly. When Carrie's mother met the teacher a few weeks later, she reported that although bedtimes were still challenging, Carrie was now getting to sleep half an hour earlier. The childminder continued to work in partnership with Carrie's mother, and gradually things improved and Carrie was less tired during the day.

Provide an area for children to rest.

To help children be alert during the day and have a healthy attitude towards sleep, you could:

- Plan activities to make most use of times when children are alert.
- Practise relaxation exercises regularly.
- Use brain breaks and physical activity to energize children when necessary.
- Teach about healthy sleep patterns.
- Keep diaries about bedtimes.
- Read stories about sleep.
- Do a whole group project on sleep and bedtime routines.
- Work in partnership with parents who are having a challenging time with bedtimes.
- Provide an area for tired children to rest during the day with beanbags or big cushions.
- Promote bedtime and bedrooms as a positive time and place;
- Sing lullabies and other calming songs.
- Play quiet music during some parts of the day.

Movement

A mother told of her daughter's experience at a nursery where she was expected to sit and concentrate for long periods of time:

We were in a hurry to get Corrine into a nursery soon after we moved. I realize now that we should have spent longer in the setting before we made the decision to send her. Corrine was unhappy right from the start. She just wasn't ready to sit for long periods learning her letters and numbers. Her behaviour started to become challenging at school and at home, and then she started to cry when I dropped her off. Soon she was saying she had an ailment each morning – sometimes just a tummy-ache or a headache, but in the end she would wake up every morning to tell me that she had broken her leg or her arm!

After several months, I finally decided to stop taking her and keep her at home. The following September she started a new nursery school – and loved it. The atmosphere was so different; activities were fun and engaging, and she wasn't expected to sit for ages at a task without a break. I still feel guilty about the months she spent at that nursery where she was miserable. Thankfully her teacher this year has revived her confidence and enthusiasm.

Teach playground games such as hopscotch.

To ensure that the children in your care learn through movement, you could:

- Provide ample opportunity for physical play.
- Limit the amount of time that you expect children to sit still.
- Build in plenty of short brain breaks if you have formal teaching sessions.
- Make extensive use of Brain Gym®.
- Develop brain break activities that involve smooth controlled cross-lateral movement.
- Incorporate action rhymes and games into story and circle times.
- Teach playground games.
- Organize your setting to ensure freedom of movement.
- Use music to accompany vigorous physical activity to energize children.
- Monitor individual children's activities to ensure that they receive a balance of different types of play.
- Look at your setting regularly to make sure the organization of the furniture does not restrict children's movements.
- Make sure your group area, story corner and music area have enough space for the children to get up and move during group activities.
- Give children options of where and how to work whenever possible, such as playing on the floor or standing up rather than sitting at tables.

Attentional systems

Attentional systems page 33

For many reasons, both physical and emotional, some children find it easier than others to maintain periods of sustained concentration. These physiological and emotional needs can be catered for in a variety of ways.

In the early afternoon, Samantha often finds it difficult to concentrate and focus on a task. Her energy levels are low because the amine levels in her body are at their lowest level of the day. *Amines* are the chemicals that act as stimulants to run the body and brain. Fortunately her teacher monitors the attention levels of the children in her class and provides lots of opportunities for physical movement. When Samantha takes part in a brain break activity, adrenaline is released, which helps to make her more receptive for learning.

VAK page 33

To cater for the different concentration levels of the children in your care, you could:

- Create lots of opportunity for play and freedom of movement.
- Use affirmations to help children to refocus on tasks.
- Ensure that the activities available meet the needs of individual children.
- Present literacy and numeracy sessions in VAK format to match input with a range of attentional cycles.
- Work gradually to introduce the longer sessions such as the National Literacy Strategy and monitor and treat children as individuals when gradually lengthening the session.
- Build in regular brain breaks to energize the children.
- Use Brain Gym® to reinforce learning points.
- Monitor the children's highs and lows by careful observation.
- Experiment to find the best times for activities that require greater concentration and feel free to stop or start a session when the moment is right.
- Try to work flexibly, giving the children with shorter attention spans the option of leaving the group after the first or second activity.
- Remember that you can combine literacy and numeracy plenary sessions and have them at any time of day.
- Use puppets, different voices, objects, music and sound to keep children engaged in listening.

Use puppets to keep children engaged.

Step 2: Developing emotional intelligence

Daniel Goleman[7] argues that emotional intelligence can prove to be a more significant factor in a child's future than any other measure of intelligence. The five aspects of emotional literacy that Goleman defines are: *self-awareness, management of emotions, self-motivation, handling relationships* and *empathy*.

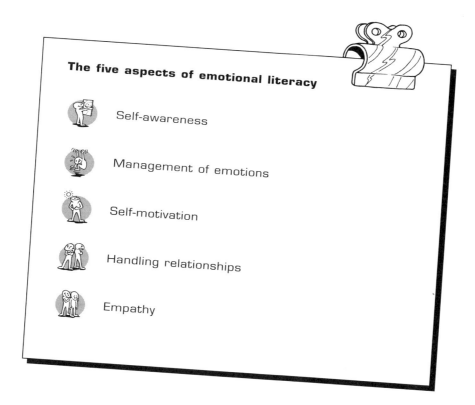

The five aspects of emotional literacy

Self-awareness

Management of emotions

Self-motivation

Handling relationships

Empathy

For full-size photocopiable version, see end of book.

One of the practitioner's main challenges is to help children to manage their emotions. Learning to manage impulsive behaviour often comes with increasing maturity, but some children need additional help to become 'emotionally literate'.

George can tend to be passive, partly because he is one of the youngest in the group. His play is not always purposeful, and he is not resilient in the face of difficulty. George will happily let other children take the lead and make decisions for him. His key-worker often creates situations where George has to lead the group and make decisions for himself. If George is not involved in positive decisions about his learning, he will not develop the attributes of resourcefulness or confidence.

Kishan, on the other hand, is certainly not passive! He is resilient and assertive, but he does not act responsibly when he rushes to grab the red tricycle first and knocks down Samantha in his wake. Kishan's teacher gently directs him to help Samantha up and check that she is not hurt before returning to the tricycle. She is encouraging him to demonstrate empathy on this occasion. Her aim is to help Kishan to become more responsible and deliberate in his play, so that he will think through the possible consequences of his actions and act less impulsively.

A father spoke of being somewhat surprised when he discussed his son's behaviour with his teacher:

When Tommy started school, the teacher spoke to me and told me she was concerned about his aggressive behaviour towards the other children. I wasn't surprised that he often shouted and so on, because everyone in our family has a bit of a temper – we joke and call it the 'Smith temper'. But I was upset to hear that he was taking it a step further at school and hitting other children.

The teacher asked if I thought that a temper was inherited, not a learned trait. That set me thinking. Of course, Tommy had seen temper tantrums in our house regularly since birth. They are never really serious, and the adults know that we may shout and stamp, but we don't hurt one another. But Tommy wasn't making this distinction. I realized that we as adults were not acting very maturely, and we were passing that on to our children.

Suffice to say that we all made more effort from then on to control ourselves when we were frustrated. We worked hard with Tommy to help him develop better self-control, and gradually he learned to use words to express frustration, rather than losing his temper.

Some strategies for helping children to develop emotional literacy

Scenario: Paula finds it difficult to wait her turn for toys such as bikes and trucks.

Strategies might include:

- Using a sand timer so that she can see how long she needs to wait;
- Redirecting her to another game while she has to wait;
- Giving out tickets or tags like those given at delicatessen counters;
- Talking to her prior to the play session about how she might need to wait;
- Helping her to verbalize her feelings about the need to wait;
- Acknowledging her feelings about waiting and using affirmations that she is very patient;
- Talking about how she waited patiently at plenary sessions;
- Using a big whiteboard or flip chart for her to 'write' or stick or draw a sign for her turn;
- Having a ticket collector with a badge, hat and clipboard to help the children to organize themselves.

Scenario: Utpal rushes at tasks and gets upset when the outcome is unsatisfactory.

Strategies might include:

- Using the 'Plan, Work, Recall' model (cf. *The Thinking Child* page 127);
- Talking before the session about what he plans to do;
- Giving him ownership of activities by encouraging him to plan them himself;
- Sitting alongside him, encouraging him to work slowly;
- Encouraging him to pole-bridge as he works;
- Making regular affirmations that he works slowly and carefully;
- Encouraging him to work with a friend to plan a task;
- Discussing sequences and difficulties at group and plenary times;
- Drawing sequences as a group and walking these through as a story or play to get them right;
- Making sure that he knows how much time he has for planned activities;
- Making sure that he knows that there will be time to return to an unfinished activity;
- Having a place for him to put unfinished models and pictures.

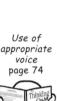

Use of appropriate voice page 74

Decibel clock page 74

Scenario: Kirsty regularly gets into conflict and shouts at her friends.

Strategies might include:

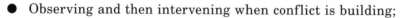

- Observing carefully what triggers the conflicts;
- Encouraging her to make friendships with less volatile children;
- Talking about the co-operative skills needed for a task before it begins;
- Structuring groups for her to work with children who demonstrate good co-operative skills;
- Observing and then intervening when conflict is building;
- Using cue cards to remind her to use an appropriate voice;
- Using the 'decibel clock' to communicate your expectations before the session;
- Practicing using different voices and talking about how it feels to be spoken to quietly or loudly;
- Making regular affirmations about how she listens to her friends and speaks gently to them;
- Practising alternative ways to handle disagreements in circle time;
- Encouraging children to be assertive and say when they don't like the noise or being shouted at;
- Praising her when she manages to control her enthusiasm.

Scenario: Jon finds it hard to read the moods of other children and respond appropriately.

Strategies might include:

- Encouraging children to verbalize their feelings;
- Role-playing scenarios in circle time where children have to guess one another's feelings;
- Reading stories that deal with children's emotions;
- Playing games with photographs of children's faces that show different emotions;
- Getting down to his level as he plays and asking him to verbalize how he thinks other children are feeling;
- Being explicit about emotions and how expressions show how somebody feels;
- Using soft toys and puppets to explore feelings and relationships.

Scenario: Christie begins activities with enthusiasm but soon loses interest and rarely completes a task.

Strategies might include:

Big Picture circle page 91

- Talking about what the task entails when giving the Big Picture;
- Discussing what the end result will be when giving the Big Picture;
- Asking her to describe how it will feel to complete the task before she begins;
- Giving regular input during a task and redirection if necessary;
- Building in regular brain breaks and opportunities for physical reprieve;
- Grouping her with children who have good concentration skills;
- Making frequent affirmations that she is good at staying on task;
- Remembering that very young children sometimes run out of steam and need an option of returning to something after a short break;
- Praising, modelling and discussing the need to take a break before returning to a task.

Scenario: Caroline can tend to be dominant and gets frustrated if other children do not follow her lead in activities.

Strategies might include:

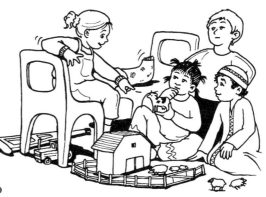

- Grouping her with children who have good group-work skills;
- Discussing who will do what before beginning a group activity;
- Observing and intervening in her play before she becomes too dominant;
- Getting down to her level and helping her to find solutions when other children do not want to follow her lead;
- Asking other children to explain to her how they feel when she is being dominant;
- Being explicit about the verbal and non-verbal cues that other children give when they are not happy about her behaviour in a group;
- Role-playing different scenarios in circle time where she can experience following the lead of others;
- Encouraging her to follow her ideas through independently when other children do not want to participate;
- Using frequent affirmations that she is good at listening to others;
- Using soft toys and puppets to explore her feelings and relationships;
- Raising the profile of listening activities in paired games, listening walks and circle time;
- Involving her in games with turns, 'conversation' type songs and rhymes, and clapping and chanting activities.

Emotional intelligence can be fostered both implicitly and explicitly. The responses that the practitioner makes to everyday situations will implicitly affect the child's emotional development, for example by helping him to manage impulsive behaviour. The lists that follow are starting points for explicit ways to help children to become emotionally literate.

Twenty-one ways to help children to manage impulsive behaviour:

1. Use *The Three A's system* of *Acknowledgement, Approval* and *Affirmation* to encourage appropriate responses to challenging situations.
2. Role-play 'what if' scenarios where children have to practise the skills of self-control.
3. Play games that involve waiting and turn-taking.
4. Use circle time to explore challenging situations.
5. When children have acted impulsively, help them to retrace their footsteps to find alternative responses.
6. Be explicit about the management of emotions.
7. Comment when you see children exercise good self-control.
8. Use role play with small world toys to illustrate ways of responding to frustrating situations.
9. Discuss the skills of self-control that are needed before embarking on an activity.
10. Play games that involve suspense.
11. Encourage children to pole-bridge.
12. Explore emotions and behaviour through stories and fantasy games.
13. Use video and photos of situations in the setting to help children explore feelings and responses.
14. Discuss pictures and posters of faces with clear expressions to help children 'read' facial characteristics and expressions.
15. Focus on both children in conflict situations. Avoid the temptation to concentrate only on the aggressor.
16. Have clear systems for cooling off, repairing relationships and returning to games.
17. Collect and use story books that explore feelings and relationships.
18. Make up your own stories that address issues about emotions and behaviours.
19. Ensure that software for the computer encourages thoughtful responses.
20. Play alongside children and verbalize your frustrations and describe how you control them.
21. Encourage children to verbalize their emotions and teach them the language that they need to describe their feelings.

Helping children to identify emotions.

Twenty-one ways to promote emotional literacy in the early years:

1. Read and discuss lots of stories that involve emotional dilemmas.
2. Stop during stories to ask what children think the characters felt and how they should act.
3. Ask children to describe what they are going to do before they do it.
4. Give lots of opportunities for role play.
5. Timetable regular sessions for circle time.
6. When children are involved in a disagreement, be interested, discuss it calmly, and help them work out solutions.
7. If a child misbehaves, help her by going back over the incident, if possible by walking it through. Ask her what she might have done differently.
8. Describe how you feel and encourage children to do the same.
9. Use reassuring language about emotions, such as, 'I bet you feel cross that....', or, 'I would think that you are upset about....'.
10. Use *The Three A's* system to help children to learn to manage their emotions and relationships.
11. Organize groups so that the more volatile children follow the lead of their more mature peers.
12. Talk about the necessary attitudes for approaching tasks before children begin.
13. At plenary sessions, talk about the way that children approached tasks in addition to what they achieved.
14. Acknowledge children's successes when handling their emotions.
15. Use the vocabulary of emotions regularly: talk about how you felt in situations and encourage children to do the same.
16. Display pictures and make books of photos of children's faces showing different emotions such as sadness, surprise, joy, fear or amazement.
17. Make a lotto matching game of faces with different expressions, using photos or clip art from your computer.
18. Include discussion of feelings when recalling or recording events on mind maps.
19. Use soft toys, puppets or small world characters to replay events and discuss how individuals felt.
20. When you read stories, talk about the expressions on the faces of characters, and discuss how they might be feeling.
21. Whenever disagreements occur, draw the children together immediately to discuss their emotions and how to deal with them.

Helping children to learn to manage their emotions.

Step 3: Providing children with the tools for learning

Fostering strong self-esteem

Self-esteem
page 38

When a child's physiological, security and social needs have been met, the next layer of Maslow's hierarchy of needs pyramid can be laid: that of self-esteem. Positive experiences help the child develop useful attitudes and tools for learning. Helping children to develop confidence and strong self-esteem is one of the most important tasks for the parent and practitioner.

Zoe was the youngest of five children. She was taken into temporary foster care after her mother became unable to care for her. She was split from three of her siblings and moved to a different foster home after a brief period back at home. This necessitated another move to a new school. Zoe's self-esteem was negatively affected and her behaviour gradually deteriorated.

Zoe's new teacher found her to be withdrawn and quiet. She contacted her previous school and had a chat with their reception class teacher, who reported that Zoe had been an outgoing child until her mother had become ill, but had gradually lost her confidence as she moved around different homes. She felt that Zoe had begun to believe that it was somehow her fault that her mother was unable to care for her.

Armed with the knowledge that Zoe had previously been a confident little girl and that this change had occurred because of her home situation, her new teacher began to work with her to restore some of her damaged self-esteem. The classroom assistant was asked to spend regular periods with Zoe and involve her in simple routines that would give her additional one-to-one attention. She took Zoe and a friend each morning to help collect the fruit from the canteen and prepare the snack.

She gave her the jobs of filling the water jugs for lunch and helping to get the reading books out of the teacher's cupboard during register time. During all these activities she used positive language to build Zoe's sense of self-worth. Slowly, she built a trusting relationship with Zoe and began to see her self-esteem increase. It would be a long time before Zoe's family life regained some stability, but for now, it was important that she experienced successes in one-to-one relationships elsewhere.

In spite of pressure from some of her family and friends to 'make Carrie independent' before she started school, Carrie's mother did not aim to foster independence at this stage, wisely realizing that before independence a child needs to experience a strong and healthy dependence.

When Carrie started in the nursery class, she found it difficult to say goodbye to her mother. She preferred going to her childminder's house, where she benefited from the familiarity and routine. Carrie's mother took her time settling Carrie into the new setting. The practitioners encouraged her to stay with Carrie for several sessions before leaving her for short periods. They took photographs of Carrie in the nursery with her key-worker, which she took home and put on her bedroom wall. They asked if she'd like to bring a favourite soft toy to school with her, and on the first day that her mother left her, she kept her teddy bear close to her. Her childminder collected her half an hour before the end of the session and spent some time looking around the nursery with Carrie so that they would have plenty to talk about over lunch.

Gradually, Carrie became more confident in the setting. She was proud to be a 'big girl' and go to 'school' like her childminder's daughters. Her self-esteem grew from her success in confidently handling the transition. She had made a good start to her school career, and the staff continued to build upon the strong self-esteem that Carrie's mother had fostered from birth.

A teacher told about a child in her class who was seen by the educational psychologist as part of a formal assessment of his special needs:

Jamie had a very rough history. He had been put up for adoption at the age of three, and from that point had been in foster care. After a failed adoption, he returned to his original foster family and was admitted back into our nursery class. Jamie's self-esteem was now at its lowest ebb: he seemed to have taken the failed adoption as being confirmation of his lack of self-worth.

The most enlightening aspect of the formal assessment was when the educational psychologist told me what he had said about himself. She had asked him what he liked most about school, about his foster family, his friends, and then what he liked best about himself. He had told her a lot of things that were good about school and the people in his life. But when she asked about himself, he could not think about one thing that he liked. Not one thing. When the psychologist prompted him by talking about what she knew were his positive attributes – his drawing ability, his loving nature, his imagination, and his sense of fun, he put his hands over his ears and wouldn't listen. We realized that it would take major work to reinstate any positive feelings that this poor little boy used to have about himself.

Twenty-one ways to foster positive self-esteem:

1. Use children's names when addressing them.
2. Get down to children's level and make eye contact as you greet them.
3. Ask children to demonstrate new skills at plenary sessions.
4. Encourage children to talk about their accomplishments at plenary sessions.
5. Tell parents and carers little details about children's successes during the day.
6. Use regular affirmations about individuals and the group.
7. Timetable regular sessions for circle time.
8. Send children to the office, another class or another group to talk about their achievements.
9. Take photographs of children succeeding and display them prominently.
10. Send notes home about children's achievements.
11. Make a 'Celebration Board' with banners and balloons where you can pin notices and pictures about children's successes.
12. Give children big badges to wear for silly awards like the 'Do-er of the Day' or the 'Worker of the Week'.
13. Use a 'can do' cap to celebrate success – the successful child gets to wear the cap for the session.
14. Encourage children to talk about their outside interests and activities.
15. Create a board for children to display pictures and stories about their friends and families and their activities.
16. Select a piece of uplifting music to play at the end of every week after talking about everybody's achievements. Get up and dance together to the music!
17. Report successes at gatherings such as assemblies or parents' meetings and give children a round of applause.
18. When a child overcomes a difficulty or makes a new discovery, ask those around him to give him a clap or a handshake.
19. Make up a celebration rhyme, chant or song with the children to use when somebody or the group is successful.
20. Create an award that you give out at the end of each week for the child to take home for the weekend and have a ceremony like the Oscars when you give it out.
21. At the end of a really successful session, line the children up and go down the line giving each child a hug, a handshake or a high five.

Circle time

One of the most effective ways of promoting self-esteem in young children is the use of circle time. Circle time fosters strong self-esteem and positive attitudes towards learning. Two basic rules can be taught to the children: nobody is allowed to interrupt the speaker, and they can only say positive, kind or thoughtful things about one another. After a warm-up time, a wide variety of activities can follow. Circle time can be used for children to revisit difficult situations, to find solutions to problems, to share their successes and to express their feelings and develop empathy for others. Alongside the social and emotional learning that takes place, circle time can provide many opportunities for the development of listening skills.

Six warm-up activities for circle time:

*Circle time
page 40*

1. Welcome ball
   One child starts by tossing a 'koosh' ball or a beanbag to another child, saying, 'Welcome' followed by his name. That child then tosses it to another, welcoming him, and so on, until everyone has had a turn.

2. Sitting down game
   Everyone stands up. The practitioner says to one child, 'Sit down' followed by his name. That child then invites another child by name to sit down, and so on, until everybody is sitting down.

3. Double hand shake
   The first child turns and shakes both hands with the child to her right, then the next child passes on the double hand shake to the child on her right, and so the double hand shake goes round the circle.

4. Cross over
   One child starts by putting his right hand across his body into the left hand of the child on his left, who then crosses his right hand to the next person's left hand, until everyone is joined with crossed arms. This takes some time to master!

5. Rope circle
   One child holds the end of a long rope or a piece of string. She feeds it through her clasped hands to the next child, who feeds it on through her hands to the next, until the rope is in a circle through every child's hands.

6. Watching, watching
   The practitioner uses a puppet to do actions that the children copy, whilst singing a song like this one, which is sung to the tune of 'Frère Jacques':

Watching, watching, watching, watching,
Copy me, copy me,
Everybody do this, everybody do this,
Just like me, just like me.

Twelve activities for circle time:

1. Welcome song

Once the children have settled for circle time, they sing a welcome song together, such as the one below, which is sung to the tune of 'Skip to My Lou'. The practitioner should encourage all the children to look at the child being named and smile as they welcome him or her. They continue the verses until every child has been welcomed by name, if necessary ending with, 'Hello, children, how are you?', 'Hello, teacher, how are you?' or 'Hello, mummies, how are you?' until the final verse is complete.

Hello (name), how are you?
Hello (name), how are you?
Hello (name), how are you?
We're so glad to see you!

2. Musical chairs

The practitioner arranges a circle of chairs, with one more chair than children. She stands in the middle of the circle and makes a statement such as, 'People who like to draw pictures,' or, 'People who like to play in the home corner.' Children must decide if the description matches them. If it does, they must get up and find another seat; if it doesn't describe them they stay in their seat. In a variation of this game the practitioner can read from cue cards that she has prepared about the week's work, for example, 'People who did cookery' or 'People who helped build an amazing model of a Tyrannosaurus this week'.

3. The picture frame

The children pass around a cardboard picture frame which they take turns holding in front of their face. While they are holding the picture frame, they can either say something positive about themselves to the group, or the other children can be asked to say something about them. These could be general comments or a specific theme could be chosen, such as 'What games I am good at' or 'What I like to do at weekends'.

4. Guess who?

The children pass around a speaking object. Then two other children go behind the screen of the book corner. One child speaks, either choosing what he or she says, or saying a set phrase that the children have already agreed upon. It can be powerful to use an affirmation such as, 'Our group is good at listening to one another.' The child with the speaking object has to guess which of the two children spoke. If they are right, they are one of the next pair to go behind the screen after passing the speaking object to the next child.

5. The message

The practitioner starts a message around the circle by whispering in the ear of the child next to her. That child whispers it to the next child, and so on, until it gets back to the beginning.

6. Run around

Once everyone is sitting in a circle the practitioner makes a statement such as, 'Wearing a red shirt.' Everyone with a red shirt then gets up, runs round the outside of the circle and back to their place. The game then continues with other categories such as items of clothing, preferences such as, 'Likes marmite,' or details about appearance.

7. Make a face

Using some pictures of faces with expressions, children take turns to take a card and without showing it to the others, make the expression. The others try to name the expression.

8. The voice

The practitioner makes a tape recording of different adults or children from the setting while they are talking. She plays extracts and asks the children to identify the speakers.

9. Say something nice

As they pass the speaking object around the circle each child says, 'Something nice was when.....' This can be extended to 'Something nice I did,' or 'Someone was kind to me' or 'Thank you to my friend Priya for....'

10. Send a movement

The practitioner starts by making a movement with her hands, such as wriggling fingers, clapping or clicking. She turns to the next person and passes the movement on, and that child copies it, then 'sends' it around the circle. New movements can be added as the first movement comes back or while the first is still on the way round. (This is much more difficult!)

11. Change places

The practitioner chooses one person, who calls someone's name and changes places with him. That child sits down, then gets up quickly and calls somebody else's name to change places with. He sits down quickly, then calls out someone else's name and changes places with him, and so on, until everybody has had at least one turn.

12. Make me laugh

One child is chosen to be in the middle. The children sing the song below and then try to make him laugh without touching him. When he laughs, he chooses another child to take his place.

We'll make you laugh, giggle giggle
You'll lose your frown,
We'll make you laugh, giggle giggle,
When you sit down.

(sung to the tune of 'Lavender's Blue')

Six activities to end circle time:

1. Pass a smile
   The children turn to each other in turn, passing a smile around the circle while singing this song:

   Turn your head and pass a smile

   (shake a hand, touch a toe, and so on)

   Pass a smile, pass a smile

   Turn your head and pass a smile

   Round the circle.

   (sung to the tune of 'London Bridge is Falling Down')

2. If I were...
   The children take turns to say what they would choose to be if they were something from a category that the practitioner picks, such as 'If I were an animal, I would be a (rabbit/giraffe/tiger).'

3. Melting statues
   The children stand still like statues and gradually melt to the ground, either to a piece of music or in silence.

4. Pass the shaker
   The children pass a shaker, a bunch of keys or a tambourine around the circle, taking care not to make a sound.

5. The candle
   The practitioner lights a candle in the centre of the circle. The children sit and watch it quietly and sing or hum a song while they reflect on their day.

6. Farewell song
   Everyone sings a farewell song such as the one below, which can be adapted to reflect the languages spoken in the individual setting[8]:

   Auf Wiederseh'n (name), Auf Wiederseh'n (name),

   Daag (name), Daag (name),

   Au revoir (name), Au revoir (name),

   Joy geen (name), joy geen (name).

   Sayonara (name), sayonara (name),

   Shalom (name), shalom (name),

   Adios (name), adios (name),

   Aloha (name), aloha (name),

   (sung to the tune of 'Frère Jacques')

Developing the 'can do' attitude

One of the keys to success is to have self-belief. This strong self-belief gives children a 'can do' attitude towards all aspects of learning. A child with the 'can do' attitude is persistent and meets challenges with confidence. He is able to work and play independently. He is likely to develop good social skills and so will then benefit from group-work activities. Providing an environment with the right level of support and challenge will help children to develop this 'can do' attitude, which is one of the keys to effective learning.

'can do'
page 43

When Samantha's tower of bricks collapses for the third time, she does not blame the other children, nor does she give up. Instead, she says, 'Uh-oh!' and pulls a silly face. Then she starts building again, this time with the largest bricks at the base of the tower. She is bolstered by a positive self-image and high self-esteem. Samantha is both resilient and persistent. She also knows how to ask for help. When her friend Angie walks by, Samantha calls to her. Angie sits down and helps her to gather the larger bricks, and together they build a tower that is tall enough to satisfy Samantha's ambitions.

At a nursery school, the children wanted some new shelving to display their models. The practitioners took them to a store to choose and purchase the shelving. They then gave the children ownership of deciphering the instructions and constructing the shelves. Unfortunately, however, some pieces were missing from the pack. But instead of the adults taking over, they helped the children themselves to phone the store to complain. The result was that the store manager came later that day to personally deliver the missing pieces!

Twenty-one ways to foster the 'can do' attitude in the early years:

1. Create lots of tasks and activities that have no 'correct' answer.
2. Create 'have a go' times, and model 'having a go' yourself.
3. Explore the idea of failure and be explicit about being 'stuck'.
4. Ask children to consider 'what if?' questions.
5. Do exercises that involve considering the outcomes of various scenarios.
6. Involve children in writing the day's or week's To Do list.
7. Give children responsibilities such as caring for the pets and organizing the book corner.
8. Set tasks that involve children thinking of lots of really good questions.
9. Set tasks that necessitate asking other people questions.

Group-work
page 114

10. Rehearse and practise appropriate behaviours such as stopping and thinking, or talking to a friend or adult.

11. Encourage children to work together in pairs or groups.

12. Notice and make a positive comment when children help one another.

13. Give public acknowledgement for 'can do' attitudes.

14. Remember to tell parents and carers about children's successes.

15. Use puppets and stories to explore positive attitudes such as teamwork and perseverance.

16. Encourage children to tell about helpful friends.

17. Talk about positive attitudes at plenary times.

18. Encourage children to pole-bridge.

19. Pole-bridge yourself, verbalizing when you make a mistake or need to rethink.

20. Collect books and tell stories about people who have overcome difficulties and have a positive attitude.

21. Create a 'can do' board where you display photographs and captions of all the children's positive achievements.

We 'can do' it: we care for our pets.

Turning negative self-talk into positive self-talk

The following five scenarios show the difference between negative ⊖ and positive ⊕ self-talk. The practitioner's task is to help children to develop the positive language that will enable them to tackle a challenge successfully.

Step 4: Managing behaviour positively

When we consider the behaviours that we wish young children to display, the first requirement has to be that we are providing a curriculum that meets their social and intellectual needs. We then need to decide what our expectations are, making them appropriate to the age and developmental stage of the children in our setting. A variety of strategies can be used to manage behaviour positively; one of the most useful being *The Three A's* system of *Acknowledgement*, *Approval* and *Affirmation*. The four-to-one rule, where four positive comments are made to every neutral one, and negative comments are avoided, is another good system for monitoring that behaviour management is positive.

Examples of good rules for the early years:

- Help to put away the toys at tidy-up time.
- Hang up your apron when you take it off.
- Put the pencils back on the shelf when you have finished drawing.
- Put the caps on the pens after you have used them.
- Help other children.
- When the timer rings, let someone else have a turn with the bike.
- Put the books back in the rack after you have read them.
- Flush the toilet and wash your hands when you have been to the toilet.
- Tell Mary before you go outside.
- Touch other children gently.
- Always look at the person who is speaking to you.
- Walk when you are inside.

Activity: auditing your interactions with children

Here is an activity to help you to analyse how you divide attention between the children in your setting.

Sit down, either alone or with your co-workers. Write down all the children's names and then make some notes about what they did last week. What did each child achieve? What did they struggle with? What did you help them with? Who demanded most of your time?

Then ask yourself these questions: What did you find easier to recall? Did you have to think hard about some of the children to remember exactly what they achieved?

Did the words simply fly from your pen for others? Was there a difference between the boys and the girls? Is there a difference between the various aged children in your care? Who takes most of your time? Is this always the same or does it vary? What actions might you need to take to ensure that all children receive your attention?

Developing intrinsic motivation and learning to learn

The intrinsic motivation to learn is one of the greatest tools that a child can have. It will enable him to overcome difficulties, be persistent and see failure as a part of the learning process. The aim of the practitioner should be to minimize the child's dependence upon extrinsic motivators and foster his natural instinct to learn from a stimulating environment.

The four requirements for the development of intrinsic motivation:

Researchers Mark Lepper and Melinda Hodell identified four essential requirements if children are to develop intrinsic motivation.[9] These requirements are *challenge, curiosity, control* and *fantasy*.

 Challenge: The task for the practitioner is to design a range of activities that are far enough within the comfort zone to make the child feel competent, yet far enough outside the comfort zone to challenge her to achieve more. The level of challenge has to be high enough that she is motivated to achieve the task, but the task must not be too difficult, or it will fail to engage her and may diminish her self-motivation.

 Curiosity: In order to evoke strong curiosity, children need to undertake activities that challenge their current level of understanding. If an activity challenges the child's sense of equilibrium, he will be prompted to fully engage in learning to resolve the discrepancy. Again, the level of challenge must be appropriate, as a large discrepancy between what the child understands already and what is presented through the activity will be likely to discourage him from engaging fully in the task.

 Control: Children need to have shared ownership of the curriculum and be free to make choices in their learning in order to make meaningful choices and become fully engaged in learning.

 Fantasy: Through fantasy and play, children have the opportunity to explore issues and emotions, which in turn can lead to increased intrinsic motivation.

The Three A's

The Three A's are a tool for the practitioner to use to encourage good behaviour and attitudes. The A's stand for: *Acknowledgement, Approval* and *Affirmation*. They form a whole feedback strategy that gives the child specific information about what he has achieved, and involves him in dialogue about what might happen next. *Acknowledgement* lets the child know that you have noticed what he is doing. *Approval* can be used, if necessary, to give the child an incentive to continue or repeat the successful behaviour. *Affirmation* explicitly states that the child has the skills and ability to be successful: that this incident was not a fluke and that it will be repeated.

The Three A's page 51

Before Kishan started school, he attended a day-care centre. At first he found it difficult to stay at any activity for more than a few moments. He would rush off before finding out what an activity actually entailed. One day a parent brought in a butterfly box so that the children could watch the life cycle of caterpillars and butterflies. Inside the box some caterpillars were eating their way through leaves and Kishan joined his friend Paula to watch them. But after a few seconds, he started to move away. His key-worker noticed this and gave the two children some magnifying glasses to look at the caterpillars' mouths. 'That's great that you're looking so closely, Kishan,' she said, and asked, 'what can you see?' He picked up the magnifying glass again. 'Umm – they've got little teeth!' he exclaimed. 'You're right, you are very good at using the magnifying glass,' she replied.

Kishan was inspired to stay for longer and look more closely at the mini-beasts. His key-worker then encouraged the two children to use the books that she had displayed nearby. Kishan and Paula read *The Hungry Caterpillar* and then decided to paint pictures of caterpillars. When she returned to see what Kishan had painted, his key-worker made the affirmation, 'Kishan is really observant. He notices lots of details when he looks at the mini-beasts carefully.'

A practitioner told the story of how a mother spoke to her before the pre-school's fun-sports day:

She told me that she was worried about Karin taking part and so was considering keeping her off school on fun-sports day. Karin is a really enthusiastic, confident little girl, and she had really enjoyed our practice that afternoon for our dressing-up race. It was made even worse by the fact that her mum spoke to me in front of Karin.

I asked her why she thought there was a problem, thinking that Karin had a dental appointment or something. But her mother's reply was, 'Oh, the girls in our family are no good at sports. She'll come last and will cry.' I explained to her that firstly, the race was a team game and that we were not emphasizing winning or losing, and that all the children were to receive stickers for taking part. I told her that, in fact, it wasn't even going to be a competition – it was just a fun activity.

The irony was that although Karin doesn't have the best physical skills, she was not the least bit worried about the sports day until her mother spoke to me. The sad thing is that if her mother persists in such negative talk, Karin will probably grow up to be 'no good' at sports just as her mum predicts.

The practitioner made sure that she used many positive affirmations about Karin's ability in the dressing-up race over the next few days, so that any damage done by her mother's description of the family's weakness at sports would hopefully be negated in Karin's mind. She also focused on encouraging all the girls to participate more frequently in physical activities, and emphasized their achievements through frequent affirmations. 'Look at those girls climb,' she would comment when Karin and her friend reached the top of the climbing apparatus, 'Karin and Bethany are very strong climbers!' She continued to address Karin's need to improve her physical skills, but did so while affirming Karin's capabilities. Gradually Karin became more confident about physical activities and her skills improved more rapidly.

The language of acknowledgement:

- I like the way that Johannes......
- Thank you Chen, for......
- I'm so pleased at the way that Kimberley......
- That was so thoughtful, the way that Red Group......
- James, I noticed how you......
- I think that we should all thank Bryan for......
- Look at the way that Sam's group is......
- We all noticed how quietly the Blue Group......
- Amina and Jake told me how you helped them when......
- John's dad told me how you both......
- I just heard that Bruce has......
- When we were clearing up I saw......

Ten ways to show approval:

1. Give a 'thumbs up' signal from across the room.
2. Give a hug with a whisper of how proud you are.
3. Give a pat on the back.
4. Give strong eye contact and a smile.
5. Tell a nearby practitioner what you noticed the child achieve.
6. Mention the achievement at the plenary session.
7. Tell the child's parent about his achievement at the end of the session.
8. Shake the child's hand.
9. Draw a smiley face on the child's hand.
10. Write the child's name on the whiteboard to remind you to tell his mum.

Twenty-five simple affirmations:

1. We can all find our own coats.
2. We take care of books and toys.
3. We listen quietly at story time.
4. We turn and look at Sandra when she speaks.
5. We pour our drinks of water very carefully.
6. We all line up quietly.
7. We pick up toys when we have finished with them.
8. We put the caps back on the pens.
9. We walk quietly in the line.
10. We put our snack plates in the dishwasher.
11. We take turns with the bikes.
12. We peg our boots together when we take them off.
13. We hand round the snack tray carefully.
14. We stroke the rabbits very gently.
15. We help our friends up when they fall over.
16. We keep our hands still when we sit on the mat.
17. We wash our hands after we have used the toilet.
18. We turn the pages of books very carefully.
19. We brush our teeth after meals.
20. We look at people when they are speaking.
21. We wipe our feet on the mat before we come inside.
22. We hold hands when crossing the road.
23. We carry scissors carefully.
24. We use a tissue for runny noses.
25. We face the front in assembly.

The affirmation, 'We stroke the rabbits very gently.'

Step 5: Fostering partnerships with parents and carers

> *Parents are a child's first and enduring teachers. They play a crucial role in helping their children learn. Children achieve more when schools and parents work together. Parents can help more effectively if they know what the school is trying to achieve and how they can help.*

Department for Education and Skills[10]

The stronger the partnership between parents, carers and practitioners, the more effective the education can be. It is important to create strong formal and informal systems for communication. Whatever the stresses or pressures of the day ahead, a wise practitioner is available to welcome parents and their children at the start of each session, and if possible, to personally say goodbye to them as they leave at the end of the day. It is also important to give parents regular opportunities to discuss their children's progress in private. Children who know that their parents and practitioners are working together as a team can be relaxed, confident and secure in the learning environment. They are more likely to develop the 'can do' attitude, develop strong self-esteem and reach their full potential.

Partnership with parents and carers page 55

George's mother was worried that he would be teased when he started wearing glasses. She came in to talk to his key-worker, who listened to her concerns, and responded:

I could see how George might feel nervous about wearing them – he really doesn't like change, does he? But don't worry, we have just the thing. Our wizard puppet has a pair of glasses for just these occasions. He will remind the children why some people have to wear glasses and tell them about famous people who wear glasses, such as Harry Potter! We also have two books in our special collection about children wearing glasses. Would you like to borrow them?

George's mum immediately felt supported. The practitioner had taken her concern seriously. She understood why she was concerned, especially as George did not like having to deal with change. The relationship between the practitioner and George's mother was strengthened through this interaction.

In one setting, a group of parents landscaped part of the play area, including a garden. Groups of volunteers worked outside, enlisting the children's help when safe and appropriate. One mother visited local hardware shops and garden centres to ask for donations of materials and plants, whilst another was simply in charge of refreshments – along with a group of children, who enjoyed carrying trays of cold drinks out to the workers. The result was not just a beautiful new play area and garden, but also a building of positive relationships and morale within the community.

Twelve ways to communicate with parents and carers:

1. Ask a group of parents to help to maintain the notice board.
2. Let the children help to make and pin up notices on the notice board.
3. Make flyers about activities and events. Get the children to colour them.
4. Create flyers with pictures on the front, or cut out in the shape of animals or toys.
5. Make newsletters based on pictures, with one snippet of information in each part of the picture (see also Appendices pages 149 and 150 for full-size photocopiable versions).

6. Ask a group of parents for help in writing the newsletters – they will know how to make sure your messages get read.
7. Get the children to paint the background for posters on big sheets of paper. Then use black paint or a thick marker pen to write the message on top.
8. Use photos, and a video or audio tape of the children – play the tape by the notice board at home time.
9. Make an 'A' frame display board or use a flip chart. Put it outside the door or in the foyer and change the posters regularly.
10. Announce daily activities, such as cooking, outings, special events and visitors, on a whiteboard or pinboard placed near the door.
11. Use the same board at the end of the session to display reminders and To Do lists for tomorrow.
12. Keep a phone list for giving messages to those parents who don't come to the setting to drop off or collect their children.

Activity: assessing how welcoming your setting is to visitors

Find a volunteer to visit the setting and then give brief answers to a range of questions. A photocopiable list of questions is included in the appendices. Alternatively, create your own checklist of questions that suit your setting. A simplified, shorter checklist such as the one shown here could be used for new parents to give feedback.

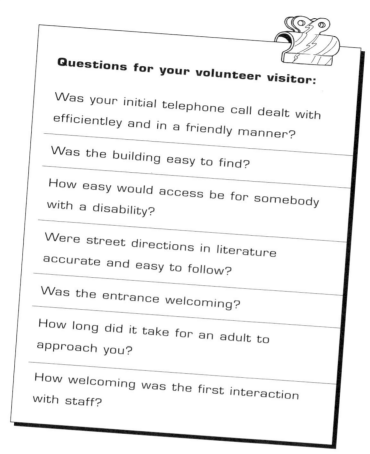

Questions for your volunteer visitor:

Was your initial telephone call dealt with efficientley and in a friendly manner?

Was the building easy to find?

How easy would access be for somebody with a disability?

Were street directions in literature accurate and easy to follow?

Was the entrance welcoming?

How long did it take for an adult to approach you?

How welcoming was the first interaction with staff?

For full-size photocopiable version, see end of book.

Fifteen good subjects for parent workshops:

1. Early literacy skills.
2. Helping your child learn to read.
3. Early mark making and writing.
4. Healthy eating and nutrition.
5. Self-help and independence.
6. Learning maths through play.
7. Supporting play at home.
8. Dealing with behaviour problems.
9. What to do in the holidays.
10. Choosing and purchasing toys.
11. Making toys from recycled materials.
12. Cooking with your child.
13. Local trips and visits.
14. What does your child do all day in our setting?
15. How we assess children's progress.

Thirty-six ways to involve parents in your setting:

1. Painting furniture to give it a new lease of life.
2. Painting patterns, lines, pictures or games on the playground or path.
3. Cutting hardboard to make small clipboards for use in the garden.
4. Planting bulbs, seeds, hanging baskets and tubs.
5. Accompanying children on walks and visits.
6. Looking for items of interest in local charity shops and markets.
7. Making concrete stepping stones for the garden by using pizza boxes as moulds.
8. Painting sections of walls or boards with blackboard paint for chalking.
9. Sitting with children while they work on the computer.
10. Collecting or making bags and boxes for collections of toys or puppets.
11. Making story sacks and collecting the items for the stories.
12. Contributing photos, artefacts, maps, cultural items and clothing for knowledge and understanding of the world.
13. Putting together new pieces of equipment and apparatus.
14. Collecting junk mail and catalogues for language and maths work.
15. Making picture labels for boxes of equipment from clip art, catalogues or photos.
16. Listening to children read or tell stories in the book corner.
17. Bringing in photos of themselves at work, at home or doing hobbies, and talking with the children.
18. Sending postcards from holidays and visits and bringing back leaflets, luggage labels and tickets.
19. Bringing cuttings or spare seedlings from their own gardens.

Parents working with children in the garden.

20. Joining in a 'Button Week', 'Container Week' or 'Cardboard Tube Week' to collect recycled items for technology.

21. Organizing a system for the recycling of paper, glass, plastic and metals with the children. Children should, of course, be supervised when handling these materials and should not be allowed to handle glass or to touch metals that might have sharp edges.

22. Joining a charity fundraising event such as collecting used stamps or a community appeal.

23. Putting up wooden battens on outside walls and fences so that you can pin up big sheets of paper for painting or fabric for shelters.

24. Making books for children's own stories.

25. Searching second-hand columns in newspapers for toys and constructions sets.

26. Testing out new places to go for outings, drawing maps, locating toilets and picnic spots, and feeding information back to you.

Parents can help with recycling.

27. Finding special offers, bargains and discounts for the things that you need to buy.

28. Setting up a 'craft supply' shop for other parents by making bargain packs with items such as glue spreaders, offcuts of paper, and little pots of glue in photo film containers.

29. Cooking favourite recipes with or for the children.

30. Sharing different foods, fruits and drinks.

31. Organizing picnics where the children prepare their own meals.

32. Tape recording songs and stories in other voices and other languages.

33. Translating books into other languages and reading them to the children.

34. Chalking roadways or train tracks onto the playground and supervising the children on the bikes and go-carts.

35. Helping the children to build a big 'camp' out of blankets, rugs, rope and blocks.

36. Setting up and managing toy and book libraries.

Supporting independent learning

Step 1: Making maximum use of the environment

The organization of the learning environment

> *The environment is a living, changing system. More than a physical space, it indicates the way time is structured and the roles we are expected to play. It conditions how we feel, think and behave; and it dramatically affects the quality of our lives.*

Jim Greenman[11]

Each practitioner has to work within the parameters of her environment, and some settings are more ideally suited for independent learning than others. However, there are many things that the practitioner can do to optimize the learning of the children in her care, and good organization is the key. Small differences in organization can make a major difference to behaviour and can influence the standard and quality of learning that takes place.

Jill is a childminder who is preparing for her day. She lives on the ground floor of a high-rise block of flats. She minds three children – three-year-olds Bruce and Martin, and Zena, who is just four. Each morning, Jill spends about 30 minutes arranging her flat for the children, before they start arriving at 8.30 am. First, she pushes her coffee table back to the wall and pulls out a box full of construction toys, cars and a set of small world people. She then covers the coffee table with a circle of thick felt, so that bricks, cars and other toys do not damage the glass. Her kitchen table is similarly protected by a plastic cloth ready for painting, dough, sticking and cooking activities.

A reading area appears behind the sofa with comfy cushions and a shelf of assorted books, next to a role play area, which is three sides of a large cardboard box, painted with white emulsion paint and complete with door and windows cut in the sides. Dressing-up clothes in a bag, cushions, a toy phone and a plastic tea set complete the house. To encourage

independence, dough is kept in a plastic bag in the fridge; pencils, crayons and paper are in the bottom kitchen drawer; books are on the bottom shelf in the living room; and water and sand toys, fishing nets, kites and wellington boots are in the hall cupboard, ready for expeditions to the play area or the park. The children can help themselves to the things they need and know how to put them away.

Today, Jill plans to take the children outside onto her small patio to wash some dolls and dolls' clothes she has bought from a charity shop, so she puts out a bowl for washing, a low clothes line and her peg bag. She is always on the lookout for new ideas for activities that will stimulate the children's interests and help them to develop skills and become more independent. She believes that the children she looks after should be encouraged to be as independent as possible, and she meets regularly with other childminders to discuss her job and improvements she can make to children's experiences – but without turning her house into a school!

One of Samantha's favourite activities is bookmaking. The reception classroom has an area specifically set out for this activity. Children have free access to paper, card and writing materials. The teacher is always on the lookout for new ideas and materials. For example, she recently found some packs of giant pencils in a pound shop, which some of the children like to use to write giant-sized letters. Samantha enjoys using them to write as neatly as she can, which is quite a challenge!

The shelves are stocked with word books and children's dictionaries for children to check their spellings, and cue cards in boxes give keywords next to pictures that can be copied if children choose. Hole-punchers, mini-staplers, treasury tags and lengths of ribbon are available for them to bind their pages together. Alternatively, some of them choose to ask an adult to help them to use the ring binder. Completed books are often displayed in the book corner where they can be read, until children decide to take them home.

In one nursery school, the staff developed an area of the outdoor playground by using just about every imaginable type of container to create a colourful display of fruits, flowers and vegetables that the children helped to tend. Old sinks, plastic pots, watering cans, baskets and barrels were painted by parents and filled with compost ready for children to plant seeds. Plants were labelled with pictures and information about their origin and growth; tools that were safe for children to use were stored on boards at child-level; watering cans sat ready for use by the garden taps; and indoor displays described the produce that was being grown, along with books about gardening. The produce that the children grew was used in cooking sessions, with every child having the chance to sample the results of their hard work. In this way, a difficult outdoor environment was put to good use.

Twenty-five qualities that foster independent learning:

1. Drawers, cupboards and shelves are clearly labelled in pictures and words.
2. Areas are clearly demarcated for different types of activities.
3. There are sufficient storage containers for all the equipment.
4. There is room for children to move around freely.
5. There is a cosy area for sharing books and stories, where books are displayed imaginatively and can be selected easily.
6. There is an area with adequate room for whole-class or large group activities such as story time or 3D mind mapping.
7. Equipment and materials are stored within reach of the children so that they can work independently.
8. The language used by adults is supportive and assumes that children have good learning behaviours.
9. There are attractive and interesting displays that invite interaction.
10. There are individual areas for children to store their own belongings.

Mind maps page 95

Organized areas for children's belongings.

11. There are surfaces where children can leave their unfinished models or work.

12. The furniture is suited to the size and number of children in the group.

13. There is a well-resourced area for writing and mark making.

14. There is free and easy access to the outdoors.

15. Display boards are at the children's level.

16. Children are encouraged to contribute to displays.

17. Parents are welcomed into the setting for formal and informal visits.

18. A listening post and cassettes are available for children to listen to stories.

19. Not too much equipment is stored on the shelves – it's not easy to get the bottom box out of a pile of six!

20. Children are involved in discussions of how and where things are kept.

21. Protective clothing and dressing-up clothes have easy fastenings and loops for storage.

22. Children have some choice of how and where they work, such as standing or sitting, on the floor or on a table, indoors or outdoors.

23. Self-care areas, such as toileting and hand washing, are easy to access and children don't have to ask an adult before using them.

24. Children are encouraged to collect the things that they need for their projects and play.

25. Children are encouraged to ask questions, think and talk about what they are doing, and request additional resources.

Providing a surface for unfinished models.

Practitioners who work using brain-based learning techniques often find that one of the results is an increase in the confidence and ability of the children to work independently. The following list gives suggestions of some basic items that can be used to implement brain-based techniques in any setting.

Useful brain-based items:

Some of these items are more suited for use with the older, more mature children. For explanations about their use, refer to the referenced pages in *The Thinking Child.*

 A copy of the brain-based learning circle (cf. *The Thinking Child* page 81).

 A board at children's eye-level for displaying the To Do list and the Big Picture.

 A board for children to display their own pictures, captions or notices.

 A traffic light poster for checking understanding (cf. *The Thinking Child* page 82).

 A whiteboard or pinboard for displaying the Big Picture.

 A cassette or CD player with a number of music cassettes or CDs.

 Sound makers and simple musical instruments.

 Sets of affirmation posters (cf. *The Thinking Child* page 54).

 A range of hand puppets.

 A camera and plenty of spare film for recording events and successes.

 A 'decibel clock' for showing children your expectations for the noise level (cf. *The Thinking Child* page 74).

 Props for circle time activities such as hats and soft toys.

Magic wands and different types of pointers for Brain Gym® exercises (cf. *The Thinking Child* page 106).

 Cue cards for practitioners to use when leading Brain Gym® exercises.

 A list or 'menu' of brain break ideas.

 Lengths of ribbon and coloured pegs for displaying posters, pictures or mind maps.

 Posters outlining rules and 'good sitting' and 'good listening'.

 A list of movement songs and rhymes for use as brain breaks.

 A parachute and book of suitable games.

 Sticky labels for making affirmation badges.

Activity: improving the environment

Take some time to evaluate the organization of your setting, being idealistic about what you'd like to achieve. Take one area at a time: for example the home corner, the big brick area or the art area. On a sheet of paper, list all the desirable items for the area, and alongside this, make notes about how you might work towards achieving your ideal. It may be possible to obtain some of these items at little or no cost by sharing your plan with parents and the community. It does not matter if the improvements cannot be made all at once, as you can build on the plan as new ideas emerge and finances become available.

For example, here are a practitioner's notes about the improvements that she would like to make to her home corner:

Colourful rug or carpet – need a new one! Ask a store for old carpet samples?	☐
Repaint the table and chairs – parents' working party.	☐
New dolls' beds – made from wooden wine boxes, ask Mrs G. to knit blankets.	☐
Need new dolls' clothes – unpick old ones to make patterns for new sets, send out note asking for fabric and ask PTA for volunteers to sew.	
Tidy and reorganize boxes of play food, utensils, and so on – need transparent boxes – put on PTA wish list.	☐

Dressing-up clothes and easier storage for them.	☐
Scarves and pieces of fabric – note on parents' board.	☐
Box of hats – note on parents' board.	☐
Need more multicultural cooking items – put on PTA wish list.	☐
Need a real cordless telephone, radio and so on – note on parents' board.	☐
Then...... have regular sessions with the children to model how to tidy up!	☐
I must remember to do a session with the whole group when I introduce a new focus for this area. They seem to need help in knowing exactly what to do and how to behave. Perhaps I should plan to spend more time there when the focus is new?	☐

A well-organized environment will encourage children to work independently. When children can take care of most of their own needs, time is not wasted waiting for adult assistance. Children can then be creative, for example by combining unusual materials in their play. By providing a well-organized environment and teaching children how to use materials, independent learning is fostered.

Children should be able to select materials independently.

Twenty ways to organize the environment to foster independence:

1. Label boxes or drawers with pictures or photographs of the contents.
2. Use clear plastic containers to store items.
3. Organize the garden shed to provide children with easy access to the equipment.
4. Provide equipment that is very flexible so that it can be used in many ways.
5. Provide clipboards and small whiteboards for children who choose to record their play.
6. Ensure that aprons and dressing-up clothes have simple fasteners.
7. Provide a low-level mirror in the bathrooms for children to check their appearance.
8. Provide footstools at sinks for children to wash their hands or the paint pots.
9. Organize the writing and bookmaking materials so that children can access them freely.
10. Cover shelves with paper and draw outlines of the pots and containers that go on them.
11. Teach children how to hang their paintings on the drying rack.
12. Provide a shelf or table for unfinished models.
13. Encourage parents to help their children remove and put on coats independently at the beginning and end of the day.
14. Use clear plastic wallets and wardrobe organizers to store items so that they are clearly visible.
15. Check scissors and other tools regularly to make sure that they do the job intended.
16. Store outdoor toys where children can get them out unaided.
17. Give children a range of tools, such as pens, pencils, felt pens, crayons, brushes and highlighters, and a range of size and thickness, so they can choose the ones they need for the work they plan to do.
18. Provide baskets, bags and trolleys so that equipment can easily be taken outside.
19. Watch the children using book racks, shelves and other storage areas, and note and rectify any difficulties they might have.
20. Remind parents to think about independence when they buy clothes and shoes for their children.

Provide footstools at sinks.

Display

Display has several purposes in the early years, not least that of showing off the work that children have done and making them feel a sense of belonging and achievement. But displays should also inform, teach and challenge children to think. They should be interactive and should enhance learning.

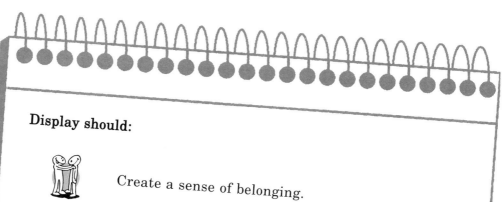

Display should:

 Create a sense of belonging.

 Enhance learning.

 Invite children to be interactive.

 Stimulate further thinking.

 Help children to make connections between concepts.

 Motivate towards further learning.

 Aid recall.

 Represent all the children.

 Be at child height.

 Celebrate and affirm success.

 Remind of rules and behavioural codes.

One practitioner described her school's policy on display by using a metaphor of the ocean. The tide would lap away at the edges of the displays day upon day, meaning that items would be added, taken away or moved. The displays would evolve and become more elaborate one week, then ebb away the next. But then suddenly, there would be a storm and the whole lot would be washed clean away, ready to start anew the next day.

When Carrie drew a picture of her mum playing tennis with her at the park, her key-worker encouraged her to write a caption to go up on the wall with the drawing and to read it back to her. She commented about how well she had formed the letter 'C' for 'Carrie' and how she had used a capital letter for the beginning of the sentence, but she resisted the temptation to 'correct' her writing. The purpose was for Carrie to work independently, which she had achieved. Carrie then proudly read the caption to her group at the end of the day.

Questions that you might like to address when you audit your display policy:

- What is the purpose of display in our setting?
- In what way does display enhance the learning of children?
- How do our displays look from a child's eye-view?
- In what circumstances should children's work be displayed?
- Where are the key areas for display?
- Who is the audience for displays in each area?
- Who is responsible for the displays in each area?
- Are there additional areas and space that could be used for display?
- How might mind maps contribute to displays?
- When should displays be created and by whom?
- How should children be involved in making new displays?
- How do we ensure that all the communities within our school are represented in our display?
- How do we ensure equality and representation of both genders and across ethnic groups with our displays?
- Are all the messages from our displays positive ones?
- Are all children represented through our displays?
- How do we acknowledge bilingualism and cater for non-English speakers in our displays?
- How do our displays reflect the local area and community?
- Are our displays at an appropriate height for children to view them?
- How often should we add to and change our displays?
- Do we discuss the displays with the children?
- Do we encourage the children to show the displays to their parents and carers?
- Do we encourage parents and carers to contribute to our displays?

Fifteen ideas for organizing displays in shared spaces:

1. Use free-standing boards to display work – one side can be used for interactive display and the other for children's own work.
2. Build interactive 3D displays in front of a free-standing board or a wall, using cardboard boxes of different sizes, covered with fabric or painted.
3. Laminate titles for displays so that they can be taken down between sessions.
4. Use a pin-pusher to minimize damage to notices that need to be taken down frequently.
5. Put tags with children's names on ribbons that can be hung on pegs or models.
6. Use lengths of corrugated card for displays, which can be rolled up after each session.
7. Keep clearly labelled storage boxes of artefacts.
8. Categorize books and keep them in labelled boxes.
9. Cut out letters and laminate them to make titles for displays.
10. Cut the sides from big cardboard boxes, paint them with emulsion paint and pin things onto them.
11. Hang things from coat hangers suspended from hooks or picture rails.
12. Use a clothes airer or indoor washing line covered with paper or fabric.
13. Use small Velcro® 'dots' to fix sheets of card or paper over shared pinboards or display screens.
14. Hang canes, cardboard tubes or broom handles from the ceiling and suspend pictures or models from them. (You may be able to leave these in place between sessions.)
15. Use a set of shoe pockets (the transparent sort that hang over a door) to display small things in the pockets. Move it to the inside of a cupboard at the end of the session.

An interactive 3D display.

Seventy-five themes for interesting displays:

animals	balls	bells
big and small	birds	blue (or any other colour)
bottles	brushes	bubbles and balloons
buttons and beads	camouflage	circles
clocks	cogs and pulleys	containers
dolls	eggs	eyes
favourite stories	feathers	footwear
freezing	fruits with seeds	glass jars
greeting cards	hair	hats
heavy and light	herbs and spices	holes
in the air	in the garden	jungle
kites	leaves	letters and cards
lids and tops	lights	magnets

mini-beasts	mirrors	night-time
Noah's ark	pairs	parties
pots and pans	puppets	rainbow colours
rectangles	root vegetables	rough and smooth
salad	seasons	seeds
shiny things	smells	sounds
spirals	squares	stars
story places	teddy bears	textures
things that bend	things that stretch	things that use batteries
tiny things	tools	transparent things
triangles	underwater	Watch it grow!
water	wheels	wooden toys

Resource Book

Apart from the usual pinboards, many practitioners find that they need additional space to fit in all their mind maps, posters and interactive displays. Here are suggestions of other spaces that can be used for display.

Twelve extra places for display:

1. The ceiling
2. The windows
3. The door
4. The kitchen
5. The cupboard doors
6. A washing line
7. Ribbons from the ceiling
8. A sheet hung from the ceiling
9. Corrugated card stretched between bookcases
10. The back of bookcases
11. A pile of cardboard boxes, covered in fabric or painted
12. 'A' frames covered in fabric.

Step 2: Helping children to develop good attention skills

'Good sitting' and 'good listening' page 72

Good listening skills are essential for effective learning. Some children need considerable help to learn to pay attention and respond appropriately. Listening and sitting are skills that often need to be taught, just like literacy and numeracy skills. Many practitioners refer to these skills as 'good listening' and 'good sitting'.

It is statistically likely that out of our four children, three will suffer some hearing deficit at some stage in their formative years. George frequently suffered from ear infections in his first three years. His parents did not find that he showed obvious signs of hearing deficit such as failure to respond when they talked, but they did notice that he often struggled with learning to pronounce new words, such as 'video', which he pronounced as 'bideo'. George underwent a series of speech therapy, which helped his language development and also helped his parents to better understand how to monitor his speech and help him when his hearing levels were low.

Carrie lives with just her mother in a flat. There is rarely any background noise in the home, and Carrie and her mother hold many long and detailed one-to-one conversations. Carrie found it easy from a young age to engage in conversation with an adult and could give good eye contact and read non-verbal cues of adults by the time she entered nursery class. However, she found it more difficult to participate when several other children wanted to talk. Turn-taking activities at circle time boosted her confidence in a larger group setting and helped Carrie to develop this skill.

By contrast, Kishan's home is much busier and noisier than Carrie's. His grandparents live with him, and several times a year the family hosts visitors from Bangladesh. Kishan is used to having to speak out to make himself heard in this busy household, and his teacher had to help him to learn to wait his turn in a class with more than 20 other children vying for her attention! Kishan also found it more difficult to sit still to listen and had to have the support of an adult as he practised the skills of 'good sitting' for several months before he could remain seated through an entire story time.

George, Carrie and Kishan each have skills that have evolved partly because of their personality and partly through experience, and all of them will benefit from being explicitly taught how to sit and listen effectively.

A father told us about his son's repeated temper tantrums in the classroom:

Lewis has always been an intense child. He gets very involved in what he is doing and builds really elaborate models. He plays imaginative games that involve a lot of talking about the story, singing songs and making incredible sound effects. One day the teacher asked to speak to me after school. Lewis had thrown a major tantrum at the end of the day and had hidden under the table and refused to come out. When the classroom assistant tried pulling him out, he had kicked her.

I was still not convinced that Lewis' problem was a behavioural one. At home we rarely had tantrums now that he had language to express himself. I went to see the headteacher, who suggested that the teacher began keeping a diary to note what typically set Lewis off with a temper tantrum. After a few weeks it became clear that his tantrums happened at the end of sessions, usually when he was expected to clear up and didn't want to. At home we rarely put that sort of time limit on activities. We tend to have flexible mealtimes and bedtimes, and if our children are involved in a project we let them finish in their own time. Lewis was simply not accustomed to this more rigid timetable.

The answer for Lewis was for the teacher and his father to work together. His father worked to help Lewis learn to bring a game to an end once he had been given a time warning. His teacher learned to give a signal to Lewis that the activity was due to end, and set up systems for him to keep models until the next day or to show to his dad before breaking them up. Gradually Lewis learned to manage his emotions.

Jane was in her fourth week as an NQT when her school had an Ofsted inspection. She told us:

The week before Ofsted arrived I was close to resigning. I was dreading the inspectors seeing what I felt was a lack of attention from the children. It would take me so long to get them to listen that by the time I had their attention, the session would almost be over! I often felt that I was talking to myself.

I didn't like to admit how I was struggling, because the other teachers were under such pressure, especially my mentor who was the deputy. Luckily, my nursery nurse, bless her, realized that things were not going well. At one of our planning sessions she suggested that we asked for help. At the staff meeting I spoke up, and I was amazed by the response! The teachers came up with a list of suggestions of ways to gain the children's attention. The headteacher came into the class the next day and we practised one or two of the methods until the children understood my expectations. They actually enjoyed the practice. I learned to wait until they were quiet before continuing to speak, no matter how uncomfortable it felt.

By the time Ofsted arrived I had cracked it. We still had a few hair-raising moments that week, but I waited it out and insisted that the children listened when I spoke. I learned that there are many techniques for achieving the same goal, and that having the right expectation was the most important thing.

It is important to give instructions clearly. Here are some principles for ensuring that children hear you and some interesting ways to get their attention.

Principles for ensuring that children hear you:

- Make sure that you have the child's attention before speaking.
- Position yourself in front of the child and get down to his level.
- Ensure that you can be seen by facing towards the light.
- Create systems for keeping the background noise to a reasonable level.
- Speak clearly and a little more slowly than your normal speech.
- Use whole sentences to help children to grasp the context of what you are saying.
- Pause between sentences and repeat complex sentences or words.
- Keep instructions short and clear.
- Ask the child to repeat the instruction or explain the meaning in his own words.
- Check for understanding regularly.
- Use appropriate facial expressions and hand gestures.
- Use visual cues to reinforce meanings.
- Sit where there is no distraction or movement behind you.[12]

Ten ways to gain children's attention:

1. Teach the children to recognize a piece of 'quiet music' as a cue for silent time.

2. Use a prop such as a magic wand or a soft toy as a signal to gain silence without needing to use your voice. Encourage the children to recognize the signal and respond quickly.

3. Teach the children some magic signals for silence, such as rubbing noses with palms or tummies with thumbs. Ask them to invent new signals, and make a new signal up each week or fortnight.

4. Tap the nearest child and give him the magic signal. He then taps the next child, who passes the signal on around the room.

5. Clap your hands, gradually becoming quieter and quieter until you are tapping three fingers, then two fingers, then one finger on your palm. Teach the children to copy until you silently put your hands in your lap and are ready to speak.

6. Use a tiny bell that you keep in a prominent place. When children see you reach for it, they will often stop before they hear it ring. Choose a child to tiptoe around ringing it gently until everybody is quiet.

7. Start by clicking your fingers in a rhythm, encouraging the children to copy. Move your hands in circles as you do so, growing slower and quieter until you cease and are ready to speak.

8. Tap your chin with a finger, then make a circular motion, tapping your ears, head, mouth, nose, and so on, while the children copy, until you put your hands down and start to speak.

9. Begin a Brain Gym® exercise and continue until all the children are joining in quietly.

10. Use a rhyme or song, such as the ones below.

Rhymes for gaining children's attention:

Touch your lips, touch your knees,
Touch your ears, now listen, please!

Point to the ceiling, point to the floor,
Point to the window, point to the door,
Point to you, point to me,
And turn and listen, quietly.

Hands on your head, fingers on your nose,
Thumbs on your ears, wiggle your toes,
Point to your friend, point to your chair,
Point to the teacher, hands in the air.
Hands on your head, fingers on your nose,
Thumbs on your ears, lips firmly closed.

Find a partner, find a partner,
Hold his hand, hold his hand,
Smile as you greet him, smile as you greet him,
Then sit down, then sit down.

(sung to the tune of 'Frère Jacques')

Let's all come and sit right down,
Sit right down, sit right down,
Let's all come and sit right down,
Ready for a story.

(sung to the tune of 'London Bridge is Falling Down')

Practitioner: Children, children, are you ready now?
Children: Of course we are, of course we are,
Let us show you how.

(sung to the tune of 'Baa, Baa, Black Sheep')

Six ways to acknowledge good attention skills:

1. 'I notice that Jamie is looking at Mitchell.'
2. 'Good. Jonah has his hands in his lap.'
3. 'Well done, Claudia, for waiting until I finished speaking.'
4. 'Now that everybody is quiet, I can explain what we are going to do.'
5. 'Karla has put down the bricks and is looking at me.'
6. 'Great! Blue Group is sitting down, ready to listen.'

Once children are busy playing and working, it can be a challenge to ensure that they maintain a noise level that is appropriate to the activities taking place and conducive to learning. The next page lists some ways in which practitioners can gain, and then maintain, a desirable noise level.

It is not possible to define the 'appropriate' noise level for the early years, as noise is often necessary for learning! Bear in mind that these suggestions are meant for those times when the group is going off task or becoming too noisy for productive activity to take place. Some of the suggestions are only appropriate for the older children. Also, remember that boys are more likely to find it difficult to be quiet. Try not to make it a gender issue!

Ways to gain and maintain a desirable noise level:

- Use your hands to illustrate the level of noise that is expected: wide arms mean free use of voices whereas closed hands mean silence. Encourage the children to do the actions with you and repeat during the activity.

- Use the 'decibel clock' with different types of activities described on it with the level of noise for each type of activity.

- Put individual cards on tables to show groups what type of voice would be suitable for their activity, such as a series of faces with different sized mouths: for example, closed for silence and wide open for a noisy activity.

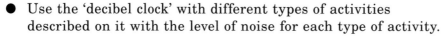

- Use frequent affirmations so that the children in your care know how to use the right 'sized' voice for each type of activity.

- Practise using different levels of voice during circle time and role-play the right noise levels for different activities.

- Use an imaginary volume control to raise or lower the volume. Let children practise turning the volume up and down so they learn what it feels like.

- Talk about 'quiet feet' and 'quiet voices' so people who are working, neighbours or others are not disturbed.

- Make a sound or sign such as a raised hand or a small bell when the volume gets too high, and help the children to respond when they notice the sign.

- Be clear when you want children to play quietly and praise them when they do.

- Limit the time when children need to be very quiet. Do it in short bursts with more relaxed sessions between. Remember that children need to talk about what they are doing.

- Have two soft toys, one who likes quiet and one who likes noise, and get out the toy that likes the noise level that you wish to establish for the activity.

Ten ways to line up:

1.   Move from one place to another without lining up, but by following a cue to walk quietly and calmly.

2.   Choose a leader and a last person, then let others join the line.

3.   Line up to an upbeat piece of music, or a quiet piece, or a foot-tapping piece; whatever suits the mood and activity.

4.   Line up pretending to be cats, dogs, elephants or giraffes.

5. Line up according to physical attributes, such as those with long hair first, followed by those with short, brown or black hair.

6. Line up with those with lace-up shoes first, then those with shoes with buckles, or those wearing sweatshirts, short or long sleeves, or caps.

7. Line up according to which activities children chose that morning: those who built with the bricks first, then those who worked in the sand tray or those who painted pictures.

8. Line up according to height, shortest to tallest or tallest to shortest. Then turn around and lead from the back, or choose a front and back leader from the middle of the line.

9. Line up according to birthdays – those who have a birthday in June first, followed by those whose birthday is in March, or May, and so on.

10. Line up in alphabetical order, then choose a front and back leader.

Lining up songs:

Ten little children made a line one day,
Up to the door and far away,
Mrs X said, 'Oh well done,
I'm so proud of you, everyone!'

(sung to the tune of 'Five Little Ducks')

We are going to the hall, to the hall,
We are going to the hall, to the hall,
So line up now beside the door,
We are going to the hall, to the hall

(or the park, story time or other destinations)

(sung to the tune of 'Heads, Shoulders, Knees and Toes')

Wind the bobbin up,
Wind the bobbin up,
Walk, walk,
Wait by the door.

Wind it back again,

Wind it back again,

Stand, stand,

Stand up tall.

(sung to the tune of 'Wind the Bobbin Up')

I hear footsteps,

I hear footsteps,

Hark don't you?

Hark don't you?

Walking very quietly,

Walking very quietly,

To the door,

To the door.

(or mat, wall or path)

(sung to the tune of 'I hear Thunder')

Heads and shoulders

In the line, in the line,

Heads and shoulders

In the line, in the line,

And eyes and nose

must face the front

Heads and shoulders

In the line, in the line.

(sung to the tune of 'Heads, Shoulders, Knees and Toes')

Let's make a line, diddle diddle,

Let's make a line,

When we are ready, diddle diddle,

Things will be fine.

(sung to the tune of 'Lavender's Blue')

Step 3: Helping children to stay on task

One of our principal aims in the early years is to help each individual child to develop good concentration skills across a wide curriculum. By providing a curriculum that is stimulating and engaging, each child should be able to spend his or her time engaged in purposeful activity. The practitioner then needs to intervene whenever concentration is waning to re-engage the children, or to adapt or expand the activity, or to redirect the children to do something new.

Kishan's teacher is often amazed by the length of time that he can concentrate on certain activities. Kishan loves to build and work in three dimensions. When working on a task that involves construction toys, he can concentrate for very long periods. Yet when his teacher wants him to draw a picture or write a short sentence, he finds it difficult to concentrate for more than a few minutes. Kishan is primarily a kinesthetic learner. His teacher needs to ensure that the paper and pencil tasks that she sets for Kishan have a purpose that appeals to him. This makes it easier for him to stay on task. For example, recently she encouraged him to draw a picture of the robot that he made from a construction kit and to write a sentence about his adventures. The classroom assistant stayed close by to make frequent affirmations about Kishan remaining on task.

In her first term Carrie found the 'big school' daunting. When the class went to assembly, Carrie sat on her teacher's knee. Her teacher would find out the content of assemblies before making the decision about whether the children should attend, and at first only kept the class in the hall for the first five minutes. Gradually she built up the time that the children were expected to stay. If Carrie or any of her friends found it too difficult to sit for that length of time, an adult would quietly bring them out. By the end of the first term, Carrie was confident and happy about attending assemblies.

Samir's childminder told us about the challenges that faced her when trying to help Samir to settle to activities for longer than a few seconds. Samir's parents explained to her that he had always been an active child. He walked at nine months and ran by nine and a half. He didn't seem to stop running for the next two years, and still preferred to be on the move. He would seemingly ignore both his mother and his childminder when they spoke to him and would often throw spectacular tantrums if they insisted that he followed their instructions.

As Samir's childminder worked with his parents to try to solve this problem, she realized that his tantrums were usually caused by the fact that he had not had sufficient time to process her instructions. Therefore what she thought was a reasonable action, such as taking his hand to make him leave his bicycle and come inside for lunch, would come like a bolt out of the blue to Samir. Once the adults began to consciously wait for a few moments after speaking to Samir, so allowing plenty of processing time before calmly repeating the request, the tantrums became less frequent and eventually ceased.

The brain-based learning circle

Brain-based learning circle page 81

This structure can be used to help those children who are ready for the introduction of literacy and numeracy sessions.

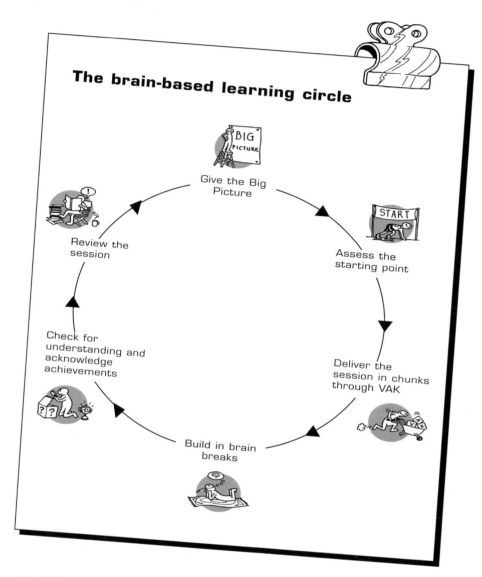

For full-size photocopiable version, see end of book.

It is important that practitioners keep in mind the developmental needs of groups and of individual children, especially when often working under pressure to cover a set curriculum in a set amount of time. Taking time to consider the questions opposite can help to ensure that the central focus remains the child, not the curriculum. The question, 'How long should a child remain on task?' should be answered with another question, 'How appropriate is the task?'

Questions to consider about how long a child should remain on task:

- Is the task appropriate for the child's needs?
- Does the task offer the right level of challenge for the child?
- What is the natural concentration span of the child, at this type of task?
- Is the child motivated to concentrate on the task?
- By what criteria would you judge the task to have been successfully completed?
- What adult support, if any, is available for the child undertaking the task?
- How frequently, and when, is feedback to be given to the child undertaking the task?
- Can the task be broken down into smaller chunks?
- Are brain breaks built into the session to give physical reprieve?
- At what time of day is the task being undertaken?
- What is the physiological state of the child as he undertakes the task?

Questions to consider when introducing the literacy and numeracy strategies:

- Are the children capable of the sustained concentration necessary for these sessions?
- Do we allow for enough variety of activity to cater for the needs of such young children?
- How are we incorporating the latest guidance and suggested activities for literacy and numeracy?
- Are we planning practical and play activities for all children?
- Are we meeting the needs of all the children in the class or group? How do we know?
- Are we offering all the aspects of communication, language and literacy to all the children? How do we check?
- Are we going to work towards completing the whole session by the end of the year?
- Do we provide for brain breaks and movement during the sessions?
- Do we monitor whether children are on or off task? What do we do about what we find?
- How do we decide which children are ready for the sessions?
- Do we introduce the sessions gradually? Do we monitor how children are coping with the sessions?
- What do we do if a child appears to be finding it difficult?
- What happens to the children who are not ready for these sustained sessions even by the end of reception class?
- When do the sessions happen? Is it always at the same time of day?
- Could longer sessions be split with a playtime in the middle?
- Could the sessions be shifted over the course of a term to different slots?
- How do we share information about the strategies with parents and carers?

Ten ways to increase children's time on task:

1. Monitor children's play carefully and intervene when they are starting to lose concentration.

2. Be ready with fresh ideas of how to restructure or develop an activity when children's concentration wanes.

3. Ask the children in a group what they might do to extend an activity and be ready to help them with gathering new materials or reorganizing themselves.

4. At the start of a session ask children to tell the group what they plan to do next and what they aim to achieve.

5. Build in review times for children to report back to the group about their last activity.

6. Use an egg or sand timer to show children how long they have spent on a task.

7. Use timed pieces of music for set tasks.

8. Build in a brain break or Brain Gym® activity when children become distracted.

9. Keep a checklist of who has taken part in a particular activity and encourage children to tick their name when they have completed the task.

10. Spend time sitting at activities yourself, even when the activity is child initiated.

In the list opposite, we suggest strategies to use as the children mature and their level of concentration improves. Some of these strategies are more suited to the older children. Younger children will need a more individual approach to developing concentration and will be working with a different adult to child ratio, where it is easier to tailor expectations and support strategies to the individual child.

Strategies to use as the children mature and their level of concentration improves:

- Observe children carefully to ascertain where and when they find it easiest to concentrate, and build on these successes.

- Stop the class or a group or an individual to ask what they are doing and what they aim to achieve next.

- Use frequent affirmations about groups and individuals, describing how they concentrate well on various activities and tasks.

- Intervene to suggest further development of an activity when you sense that children are starting to lose focus.

- Make labels for children to collect as they start on their chosen activity.

- Make labels on badges, lengths of wool or clips that children can attach to their clothing to show what activity they have chosen to participate in.

- Give challenges to groups that require sustained concentration for successful completion.

- Group children with those with greater concentration skills working alongside others who find it harder to remain on task.

- Talk about what you are doing as you work alongside children, giving suggestions of how they might extend the task.

- Use calming background music to create the mood for concentration.

Step 4: Talking the language of learning

Giving positive feedback

The language that the child hears at home and within the setting creates for him a set of beliefs about himself, which will strongly influence how he learns. Children need to hear explicit descriptions about desirable behaviours and about themselves. This sort of clear, positive feedback gives power to positive thinking, which in turn leads to high achievement.

A nursery nurse told the story of Cara, who was the fourth of six children:

Cara was four years old, going on forty. Her mum was doing her best to keep the children fed and clothed in very difficult circumstances. I had taught the three older girls, but Cara was not quiet and 'easy' like her older siblings – she was a very determined little girl! Her mum simply couldn't cope with a child who questioned her authority at every turn. When her mother arrived early one day to collect the children, Cara did not want to go. She was busy clearing up after a cookery session and wanted to stay until her biscuits had come out of the oven.

Cara's mum had clearly not thought it important to tell the children that she was going to collect them early, and she lacked the skills to negotiate with Cara about needing to leave. 'Bad girls don't get ice cream on the way home. Only good girls get ice cream,' she said to Cara as she pulled her over to the cloakroom. 'I like being a bad girl,' shouted Cara, and she grabbed my hand. 'My teacher likes bad girls too – don't you, Mrs Simpson?'

I realized that Cara simply categorized herself as a 'bad girl', whereas her older sisters were 'good girls' who deserved ice cream. Cara imagined that I agreed with her mother that she was a bad girl, but that I had no preference for either good or bad children.

I realized that we needed to be more explicit about giving positive vocabulary to Cara's good qualities and attributes. For example, if Cara raised her voice to tell another child to return a snatched toy back to a friend, we would draw more attention to her having a strong sense about fairness than to the fact that she had shouted. We started giving labels to her positive behaviours, and gradually she stopped saying that she was 'bad'. It was interesting that her dominant behaviour diminished when she was given positive labels for herself. Her mother also found her behaviour easier and their tempestuous relationship gradually calmed down.

After a role play activity, Carrie's teacher encouraged the children to discuss what they had liked about one another's 'performance'. 'I liked it when Zack pulled funny faces when he said the dinner was yummy,' said Carrie. 'Why exactly did you like that?' questioned the teacher. 'Cos he didn't really like it,' replied Carrie. 'Cos his face said it was *dis-gusting*!' chipped in another child. So Zack learned that his clowning act had been a success and that his audience had understood the difference between what he had said and what he had really thought. He learned that this technique worked and was motivated to use it again. His classmates learned something too, and some of them were inspired to try out this technique at a later date.

A reception class teacher talked about how the practitioners at her school work hard to speak only positively about the children in their care:

Our school is situated on a very tough estate, and a very high proportion of our children have free school meals. It is depressing to feel that we are sometimes expected to achieve the same by the end of Key Stage 1 as other schools in the area. Many of their children come into school already able to read. Some of the children in my class can barely speak in sentences.

Yet we try very hard to never speak negatively about our pupils, either inside or outside school. We focus on the positive. Sometimes it is difficult, but that's where you need a strong team and good support from the management. Our headteacher is always quick to pick out the positive, and she comments on progress made, rather than on scores attained. This makes an impact on the morale of the staff and has a positive knock-on effect on the self-esteem of the children.

Feedback is as important for the development of social skills as it is for academic achievements. George's key-worker had been pleased to observe that on Monday, George had walked across to the nursery without grasping her hand. George had instead walked with his friend Dinesh. She had told George how she had noticed and how pleased she was to see that he and Dinesh were becoming good friends. When it was time to walk across the playground the following Monday, George came to grasp her hand. His key-worker took his hand gently and called to Dinesh. 'Do you remember how you walked across to the nursery with Dinesh on Monday?' she asked. George nodded. 'Would you like to do the same today?' she said, putting George's hand into Dinesh's. George happily went across the playground with Dinesh. After revisiting the previous experience, George was helped to repeat his success a week later.

Remaining 100 per cent positive can sometimes be challenging for busy practitioners. The activity below can be a useful tool for auditing the language in your setting and ensuring that when you are under pressure, you don't fall into the negative trap.

Activity: The four-to-one-rule

By following the four-to-one rule, you will ensure that you use four positive comments for every neutral one and simply avoid using negative comments. This may seem a daunting task, and sometimes it takes practice to keep the language in the setting only positive. Use the chart overleaf to monitor the talk in your setting. Ask a colleague or friend to observe you and note what sort of comments you make to children during the normal course of the session. In the first column, the observer should note the names of the child or children who are involved in the interaction. Then she should tick one box to show whether the comment was positive, negative or neutral. In the right-hand column, she may wish to make a brief note to remind her of the context or of anything that she might wish to discuss after the observation.

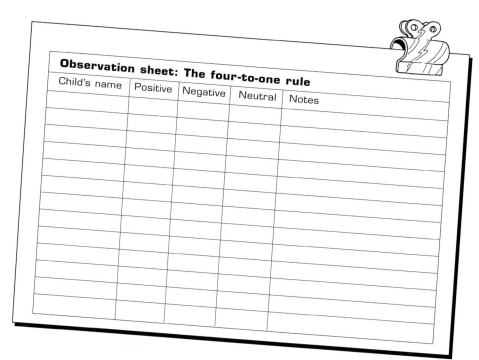

Observation sheet: The four-to-one rule

Child's name	Positive	Negative	Neutral	Notes

For full-size photocopiable version, see end of book.

Examples of neutral comments:

- 'Jamie, I would prefer to see you sit on the mat right now.'
- 'Natasha, could you show me how you put the paintbrushes carefully in the pots?'
- 'Jasmine, do you remember that we take just one snack at a time?'
- 'Andy, remember that we put our own plates into the dishwasher when we have finished lunch.'
- 'Ella, can you hang your coat up, please? That's right, it goes on the green peg.'
- 'This is the way we wipe our feet, wipe our feet, wipe our feet; this is the way we wipe our feet, before we come in from the rain.'

Seeing negative qualities as positives:

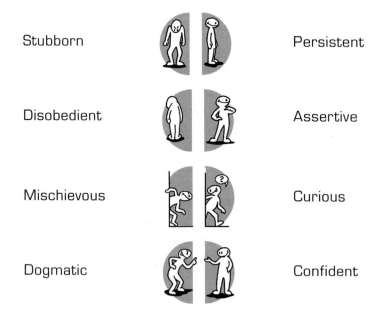

Stubborn	Persistent
Disobedient	Assertive
Mischievous	Curious
Dogmatic	Confident

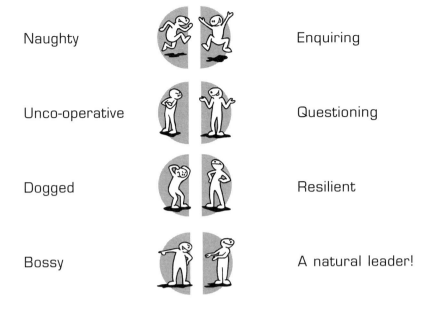

Naughty		Enquiring
Unco-operative		Questioning
Dogged		Resilient
Bossy		A natural leader!

Forty positive adjectives to use with children:

active	gentle
affectionate	graceful
artistic	healthy
assertive	helpful
calm	imaginative
careful	intelligent
caring	kind
clever	lively
confident	loving
considerate	mathematical
creative	musical
curious	outgoing
determined	peaceful
energetic	persuasive
entertaining	polite
enthusiastic	quick
expressive	scientific
friendly	strong
funny	thoughtful
generous	warm

For full-size photocopiable version, see end of book.

Activity: Positive thinking

Using a group-list such as the one on the next page, think of positive adjectives to describe each child. This will give you a good idea of the children whom it is easy to praise, and those who might get less of your positive attention during the day. Alternatively, you might prefer to brainstorm a list and then see how many of the adjectives you can use in one session with the children.

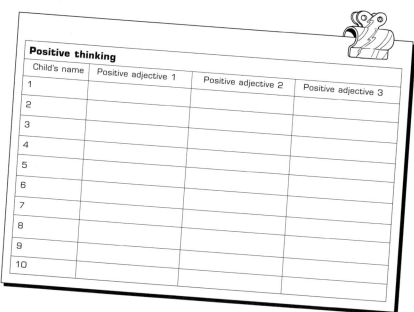

Positive thinking			
Child's name	Positive adjective 1	Positive adjective 2	Positive adjective 3
1			
2			
3			
4			
5			
6			
7			
8			
9			
10			

For full-size photocopiable version, see end of book.

Activities using positive adjectives:

These activities should be used with discretion – some younger children find adjectives confusing!

- At circle time, give each child in turn a card with an adjective printed on it. Read the word and discuss its meaning, then ask the child to give it to somebody who matches the description.

- At the end of the day, give children stickers with the adjectives written on them, to match an achievement or activity done during the day. Ask them to explain to their parents why they received that sticker.

- Before a task begins, discuss one or two attributes that might be useful and write the adjectives up on the board or a poster.

- Create fun hats with positive descriptions pinned on them, such as 'thoughtful friend', 'good listener' or 'careful worker'. When a child is particularly successful, give him the hat to wear for the rest of the session.

- Create a positive adjective board. Pin up a selection of adjectives, then put up photographs of children as they display those attributes in everyday activities.

- Say, 'I'm thinking of someone who is kind/friendly/funny', then get the children to guess who you are thinking about.

- Make a selection of character cards showing key attributes such as 'Careful Cat', 'Gentle Giraffe', 'Helpful Hamster', 'Strong Snake', 'Musical Monkey', 'Mathematical Mouse' or 'Scientific Shark', and ask the children which characters they need to help them with the work they have planned.

 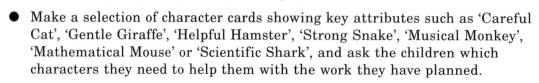

Changing negative comments to positive comments

Making positive statements or asking positive questions encourages children to learn good behaviour.

Useful phrases for giving verbal feedback to young children:

- It's interesting that.....
- I like the way you......
- I noticed that the......
- I see that this part is......
- The way that you......
- When you........I saw that the other children......
- How careful you were being when you......
- You were really thinking when you......
- You made Kerry feel so much better when you......
- Paleb felt so good when you said......
- I was looking round the garden when I saw you helping......
- Well done, you stopped to think before you......
- Good building/cutting/tidying up/helping/sorting/counting......

Useful phrases to open productive dialogue:

- Can you tell me how you.......
- What do you think would happen if you........
- Who might be able to help you to.......
- If you did this part a little differently what might.......
- Next time you do this activity what will you......
- How many ways could you........
- How would you tell your friend to do this.......
- What do you know now that you didn't know before.......
- What did you do first/next/after that?
- What did you use for......
- Who was helping you......
- Which part was the best......
- Which part did you enjoy doing most?
- How did you work out the way to......
- When/how did you learn to......
- Why did you do it like that?
- Which bit are you really pleased with?
- Show me how you ......

Pole-bridging

Language is the most important cognitive skill because it is the child's first symbol system, which is then used to learn other symbol systems such as math.

Ronald Kotulak[13]

Pole-bridging is when you talk about what you are doing, while you are engaged in an activity. Toddlers do this quite naturally as they acquire the language to describe their actions. As children get older they often become more self-conscious about talking aloud, yet pole-bridging can be one of the most effective ways of making learning concrete. Adding language to an activity helps children to process their thoughts, link concepts, challenge their thinking and commit the learning to memory.

Pole-bridging page 85

George's key-worker noticed him working busily in the book corner, sorting the books into categories. She sat down nearby and listened to him before joining in sorting the books.

'Hungry Caterpillar, now, he's hungry – very very greedy, he comes out an egg. Like ducks. Quack quack, ducks, they come out of an egg too!'
(George puts the book *Five Little Ducks* next to *The Hungry Caterpillar*)
'Oh, here's the brown bear book – yellow duck, yellow duck, what do you see?'
(George puts *Brown Bear, Brown Bear, What do You See?* next to *The Five Little Ducks*, which is now next to *The Hungry Caterpillar*. He then starts to look for other books about ducks.)

George's key-worker started to look for other books about ducks and eggs. 'Oh, here's *The Very Quiet Cricket*,' she said. 'He comes out of an egg too.' George took the book from her and put it next to *The Hungry Caterpillar*.

She then sorted books quietly, allowing George to continue his task, handing him other books that seemed relevant to his search. They worked companionably, both pole-bridging, until George was satisfied with his reorganization of the books.

To help children to learn through pole-bridging:

- Model the process yourself whenever you demonstrate how to do a task.
- Encourage all the adults working in your setting to pole-bridge as they undertake everyday tasks.
- Practice pole-bridging during circle time.
- In plenary sessions, draw attention to children who pole-bridged during the previous activity. Ask how it helped their learning.
- Draw attention to the specific language needed for an activity when giving the Big Picture.
- Prompt children to pole-bridge when you move around the room.
- Settle alongside children as they play, making pole-bridging a two-way communication as you work together on a practical activity.
- Sit down to participate in an activity yourself – do a drawing, make a model or roll out the clay, pole-bridging as you do so.
- Sit down and talk children through the activity, such as, 'Kyle, I can see how hard you are working to thread that bead. That's it, push the end of the string through the hole. Now which one next? A green one? Oh dear it's slipped! Pick it up again, that's right. Now turn it round and find the hole.'

Big Picture
page 91

Developing brain-based techniques

Step 1: Teaching children to mind map

Mind mapping is one of the most powerful tools that can be used to enrich children's learning. Young children find mapping very easy. A mind map is like a spider diagram or a flow chart, with the keyword – the topic – of the map written in the middle, supported by a symbol or picture. The map then develops from the centre outwards, with keywords or pictures joined by lines or arrows to show the connections. It can be built and rebuilt as often as children wish, as they talk through their ideas and the connections that they have made between concepts.

Mind mapping page 93

A practitioner on a brain-based learning training course told of her daughter's ability to map at the age of 13 months:

While I was pregnant I often listened to classical music. My daughter Chloe seemed to recognize my favourite pieces of music from birth. One day we had been outside in the garden, and Chloe and I had been admiring the pretty flowers. Later that afternoon I put on one of my favourite pieces. Chloe stopped what she was doing and listened intently, moving her hands to the music. 'Isn't it pretty?' I commented. 'F-f- f-ower,' she said, in a hushed voice, moving her hands delicately in the air in the way that she had touched the flowers in the garden. After that, classical music became known as 'flower music' in our household.

At just 13 months old, Chloe had linked the concept of 'pretty' from the pretty flowers in the garden to the pleasing music that her mother played in the house. She had learned to categorize the music that she heard around her, as only classical music earned the title 'flower music'. Her ability to map and make links between concepts was already strongly in place.

Carrie watched a television documentary with her mother about the plight of the elephant and how the species is threatened.

At school the next day, Carrie went straight to the technology area. She worked with concentration for almost half an hour, talking to herself as she worked. She carefully stuck together two cardboard tubes, some lolly sticks and a cereal box. She also made a small, highly decorated box, using carefully chosen items from the selection on the shelves. Carrie was making maximum gain from this activity because she was adding language to the experience. Her teacher encouraged her first to pole-bridge, then later to describe her activity to others.

At the plenary session, Carrie explained her work to the group. 'It's a submarine for rescuing elephants,' she explained, holding up her model. 'It can travel through the ocean at the speed of light. It has propellers here that spin really fast. They also work to light the way for the sailors. It can change into a land cruiser, but only when it is dark. It's on a secret mission to save the elephants from the bad men who want to kill them. I can't remember...'

'Poachers?' suggested her teacher. 'Yes – poachers!' continued Carrie, 'so the submarine takes the elephants down to a world at the bottom of the sea where they can be safe until after all the, um, the poachers have gone home. Then the wise men will teach the poachers that they must leave the elephants alone. Their wives will show them how to make beautiful jewellery, which they can sell.' Carrie held up her highly decorated box. 'See? This is the jewellery that the poachers will make from seashells. Then the submarine can take the elephants back to their land where they are safe because the poachers won't shoot them any more.'

To build upon her learning, her teacher later helped her to put her ideas onto a mind map. The teacher scribed for her as they built the mind map together. Carrie demonstrated and consolidated the pattern of connections that had been made in her mind, and used skills of sorting and of categorization. Carrie's thinking was challenged through the activity, and her teacher was able to assess Carrie's understanding as they built the map. She later used the map to plan future activities. By using mapping she helped to lead Carrie onto further learning.

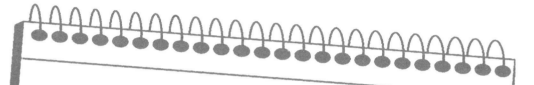

Five main applications of mind mapping:

 Assessing current knowledge and understanding

 Sharing ideas and fostering group-work

 Making connections between concepts

 Revisiting previous learning

 Challenging thinking and extending learning.

The following case studies are examples of how mind mapping can be used for five specific purposes.

Assessing current knowledge and understanding

A pre-school group is going to begin a topic on mini-beasts next term. In order to inform their planning, each key-worker spends some time drawing up a mind map about mini-beasts with their group of children. They find that there is a gap between the understanding and knowledge of the older children and those who recently joined the pre-school. In fact, some of the older children are so knowledgeable that their key-worker joked with them and started calling them 'David Attenborough'! The practitioners then planned their topic with this disparity in mind, with some more challenging activities primarily designed for the older children.

Sharing ideas and fostering group-work

A reception teacher works with a group of children to review their experiences of a fair that visited the green opposite the school last night. The teacher uses a 'fishbone' mapping format to help the children use all their senses to remember the sensation of being at the fair. Together, they think about what they heard, what they saw, what they touched, tasted, smelled and, most importantly, how they felt. The teacher helps them to record the experience on the big fishbone map using thick felt pens to make pictures and words. When they have finished the map, it is displayed on a low-level board where all the children can see it as they go off to paint, draw and make models of the fair. Some of the children begin to make a big model fairground in the technology area, while others make little books in the writing area. In the garden, groups of children use the large apparatus to re-create rides and games.

For the rest of the week, the children continue to work on the map, adding words and pictures as they share ideas in their groups. Mind mapping has enabled these children to revisit all the sensations of the fair in a safe situation. The activity has enabled them to share experiences, reinforce vocabulary and share their feelings – all preparation for reliving those experiences in the variety of play activities available.

A 'fishbone' mind map.

Making connections between concepts

Carmen is two and a half, and she is fascinated by matching and naming similar objects. She rushes into her childminder's kitchen clutching a model elephant, which she has brought from home. She goes to a drawer and begins to rummage around among the tea towels, saying 'Elephant, elephant'. She gets more and more frustrated as she looks. Carol, her childminder, asks, 'What on earth are you looking for?'

'Elephant, elephant,' says Carmen, getting more and more frantic. At last, Carol realizes what Carmen is looking for. The day before, they had been shopping and Carol had bought a new tea towel with a border of elephants! At home, Carmen's memory had been triggered when she played with her zoo animals, and she had even remembered to bring her elephant to Carol's house the next day.

Carol found the tea towel, which Carmen carefully spread out on the table saying 'Elephant, elephant, elephant', as she walked her elephant along the border, delighted to match and reinforce the two images. Later, Carol found a cuddly elephant and they played feeding it a banana. Before Carmen went home, they read *The Elephant and the Bad Baby* together, and Carmen borrowed the book and the tea towel to take home to show her mum and dad.

Revisiting previous learning

Fintan is in reception class. In the autumn term, the class spent some time learning about harvest and why farmers often use scarecrows to protect their crops. Now it is spring, and the teacher plans to do some work on growth and plants. She wants to help the children to recall what they learned previously. She starts to build a mind map with them, with the central topic being 'plants'.

After a few minutes, Fintan puts up his hand and says, 'The farmer makes a scarecrow.' 'Yes!' says his friend Bruce, 'because it can scare the crows away!' The children start talking about scarecrows and harvest, and gradually, between them, the learning that they did last year is recalled. By the end of the session, the teacher is satisfied that all the children now remember most of what was covered last year. The mind map is quite detailed and can be displayed alongside the old ones from the autumn, and added to as the project work progresses.

Challenging thinking and extending learning

A group of five year olds are preparing for a visit to the park. They go to the park in all seasons and weathers, sometimes to play and run and shout, sometimes for a particular purpose. Tomorrow, they are going to look for signs of spring. After a discussion with the teaching assistant, they begin a map, working as a group on a large sheet of paper. Their map is a representation of where they might look for evidence of spring. They draw the familiar features of the park – the paths, swings, pond, steps, buildings and other places. As they draw, they mark the places where they will look for evidence. They talk about plants growing, leaves coming out, birds and other creatures they have talked about and begin to plan a route round the park, so that they don't miss anything. They make a pictorial list in one corner of the map of things they might find at the park, and in another corner, a list of things they need to take.

The classroom assistant supports the children as they work. She also observes and assesses their knowledge and understanding of the topic under discussion, their expanding vocabulary and their emerging scientific methods. During the day, children come back to add details to the map, and collect the things they need to take with them. The classroom assistant asks questions that challenge the way that the children are thinking. 'Oh, might we find new plants there?' she asks, then ponders aloud, 'I wonder if they will grow in the playground? What's the playground made of, can anyone remember?' The children reconsider their idea that daffodils may be growing in the tarmac. 'But there might be some in the pots,' says one of the boys, drawing in the flower containers on the map. At home time, children bring their parents in to show them the map and tell them about their plans.

When the children go to the park the following day, the map stays at school, but they remember exactly what they are looking for. They look, photograph, draw and collect their evidence, which they add to the map when they return to school. Further discussions follow the visit as the children review the visit, extending their thinking by shared experience and discussion, and using the growing map as a support to their learning.

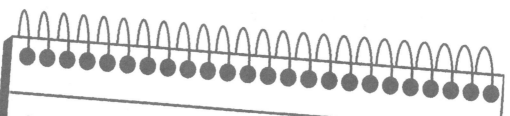

Good reasons to map in the early years:

 Young children are natural mappers – mapping utilizes their natural intelligence.

 Mapping can be used as an accurate assessment tool.

 A mind map can become a record of what the child knows and understands.

 Mapping can be used as a planning tool and a method for sharing plans with the class or group.

 Mind maps can be revisited to add new connections and concepts.

 The process of mapping fosters group learning and co-operation.

 Mapping helps children to connect concepts that otherwise would be learned in isolation.

 Mapping is a skill that will benefit children for life.

 Mapping is an active process that can stimulate all the senses.

 Mapping is fun!

Step 2: Adventures in play

One of the practitioner's principal challenges is providing the right environment for a balance of play activities. Providing opportunities for good quality play enables children to develop physically, cognitively, emotionally and socially. There needs to be a balance between child and adult initiated play; between indoor and outdoor play; and between the types of play activities. The practitioner's role is to observe, interact and provide for the development and enrichment of play activities. Sensitive intervention is an art, not a science. Successful intervention depends upon careful observation and knowledge of the individuals and groups within a setting.

Balance in play page 98

A nursery nurse described an experience that reinforced for her the importance of allowing children time and space to organize their own learning. She asked some children to help her take down a travel agent display that had a role play element. She left the area briefly to put away some fabric and books. When she returned, the children were sitting on a row of chairs, gazing at the blank wall. 'What are you doing?' she asked. They told her, 'We're at the cinema, watching *Jungle Book*. You can come if you like. Get a ticket, it's 10p.' The cinema was such a success that it remained the focus for role play for several days, with different 'films' on each day, tickets, ice cream, popcorn and ushers with torches to show the customers to their numbered places. The children's experience was considerably richer than it would have been if she had ignored their ideas and simply organized her display.

In the nursery, a group of children were busy playing with the toy cars on the mat. Carrie was working nearby, building a large construction from the Duplo® and was trying to decide what to do with it. 'What is it?' asked one of the children from the mat. 'A petrol station,' replied Carrie, and the children helped her to lift it down onto the mat. A game then ensued using the cars and the petrol station, and the Duplo® box was lifted down so that the children could extend the game. At that moment, the student who was organizing the art activity came over. 'Who hasn't done their bubble painting yet?' she asked. 'Me,' replied three of the six children. They went off with her to put aprons on. The game on the mat fizzled out, and Carrie and the other two children wandered off to play elsewhere. A well-intentioned but ill-timed interruption had put an end to independent play.

Some reasons for the provision for high quality play

The main reason for play is that, for a young child, it is work. Play is a child's method of learning about his world and processing events in his life. The following case studies are examples of how everyday play situations help children to develop physically, intellectually, socially and emotionally.

Play helps children to learn to manage their emotions

This morning 20-month-old Susie is lining up her teddy bears to feed them. First she offers a plastic apple, 'Yum yum', then a drink of water, 'Tup tup tup'. Next she offers a pretend bowl of porridge, 'No, no, no, me don't like!' squeals the first teddy. The imaginary porridge ends up on the floor. Susie is working through a scene from breakfast time, when she had decided that she would prefer a banana to porridge. Mummy didn't have any bananas. Susie had cried and thrust the porridge at her mother. She is still cross, and this game is helping her to process her feelings and make sense of what had happened. 'B'na-na later,' she tells teddy.

Susie's mother is paying attention and realizes that Susie is working through the episode from that morning. 'I know you were upset that I don't have any bananas,' she says, 'shall we go to the shops as soon as you're dressed to buy some for lunch?' Susie beams a smile at her mother. 'B'na-na later,' she says. 'Yes,' laughs her mother, 'we'll have banana later.' She validates Susie's feelings and reassures her that it is acceptable to feel anger, but that it is good to find a way to work through that anger and find a solution to the problem.

Play helps children to develop independence

TJ's favourite game at the moment is to run away whenever his mother wants him to get dressed. Although sometimes his mother gets very frustrated by this, TJ's play is serving a particular purpose in his development. He is playing out being in charge – being the adult. He is exploring how it feels to be in control. When his mum finally persuades him to get dressed, he insists on doing everything himself, thus practising the activities that he sees adults doing and learning to become independent within the security of his mother's presence.

Play helps children to practise new skills

George often acts out various situations after the event. After an incident at pre-school where he was asked by his key-worker to share the crayons with the other children in his group, he played a game where he shared out his books in piles for himself, his mum and his dad, making sure that the piles were the same height and that everybody was happy. As he did this, he was processing the earlier experience in the most natural way – through practical play activity that allowed him to experiment with the emotional impact that today's incident had upon him. 'Thank you, George, for making sure that we all had the same amount of books,' said his dad. This reinforced for George the concept that sharing is good and that it brings pleasant consequences.

Play helps children to make sense of past experiences

One of Kishan's favourite games is playing 'school'. In the evening, he often lines up his soft toys and involves them in complicated rituals, which are his versions of what he sees adults doing during the day. He acts out snack time, praising 'good sitting' and 'good sharing'. He tells stories, holding up the book so the toys can share the pictures. He leads them in singing his versions of favourite songs. This play activity enables Kishan to revisit his day, making sense and order of what he has experienced.

Play helps children to practise behaviours

One of Carrie's favourite activities is domestic play. She will set up a house in the garden at home or school, selecting a few friends to join her, using leaves for plates and flowers or stones as food. She organizes her friends, playing parent roles with extremely accurate language, tone and action. Her friends love playing with her because she is a natural mimic, and they often end up in heaps of giggles at the things she says! This type of play enables Carrie to 'try on' all the behaviours she sees at home and school – to be other people, feel what they feel, try on voices, words, movement and relationships in the same way as she might try on her mother's shoes or talk on the phone like her childminder. This is the way children make sense of the world, by playing it out over and over again with infinite variations, until they can fit it into their understanding.

Tina Bruce's definition of the 12 important features of play:

1. In their play, children use the first-hand experiences that they have in life.
2. Children make up rules as they play and so keep control of their play.
3. Children make play props.
4. Children choose to play. They cannot be made to play.
5. Children rehearse the future in their role play.
6. Children pretend when they play.
7. Children play alone sometimes.
8. Children and adults play together, in parallel, associatively, or co-operatively in pairs or groups.
9. Each player has a personal agenda, although they may not be aware of this.
10. Children playing will be deeply involved and difficult to distract from their deep learning. Children at play wallow in their learning.
11. Children try out their most recent learning, skills and competencies when they play. They seem to celebrate what they know.
12. Children at play co-ordinate their ideas, feelings and make sense of their relationships with their family, friends and culture. When play is co-ordinated, it flows along in a sustained way. It is called 'free-flow play'.[14]

Following careful observation of children's play, skilful intervention can enrich and extend the activity.

Twelve ways that an adult can intervene with good effect in play activities:

1. By joining the domestic play saying, 'I'm going to make myself some toast. Anyone else want some?' In this way the practitioner can demonstrate new activities that will enrich play, without directing it.

2. By taking the role of a waiter in a café setting, with an imaginary pad and pen, saying, 'How can I help you madam? Would you like to see the menu? Would you like juice or tea?'

3. By asking a group of children outside, 'Can you think of a way to play football together, so that you don't get in each other's way?'

4. By asking a group of children playing with the bricks, while another child hovers at the edge of the group, 'Can Jason bring his digger into your building site? I think he needs to deliver some more sand.'

5. By sitting by children in the sand and asking, 'What do you think will happen if you throw the sand?' or, 'How do you think Travis feels when you keep taking all the sand?'

6. By offering a basket of pens, small cards and playground chalk to children involved in small world zoo play, to spark interest in mark making.

7. By putting on sunglasses on a sunny day and lying down on a beach towel with a book, and then when the children show interest, asking, 'Do you want to come and sunbathe with me?'

8. By leaving surprises – such as putting ice blocks in the water tray, sequins in the sand or dried pasta in the saucepans in the home corner.

9. By offering a simple resource during play – such as some hose pipe and guttering for children experimenting with waterways.

10. By offering support without taking over, such as by asking, 'Would you like me to hold that while you cut it?' or, 'Shall I fetch you some sticky tape?'

11. By asking children if you may join their play, suggesting they should tell you what your role is and how you can fit in.

12. By giving children time and space for their games, even though this may mean reorganizing your own intentions to accommodate their interests.

Often practitioners have to work in less than ideal conditions. The following list gives suggestions for those who have to share their accommodation with other groups.

Ten ways to maximize play opportunities in shared accommodation:

1. Let the children help to set out the apparatus, following their suggestions about what should go out and where.

2. Put the equipment out in a different way and in different places.

3. Combine equipment in unusual ways, such as putting zoo animals in the water tray, gloop with cups and saucers, or lengths of ribbon or string with the bricks.

4. Use old cardboard cartons and boxes, the bigger the better! Just leave them for the children to play with and respond if they ask you to help with joining, cutting, painting, sticking or fixing.

5. Cut big boxes such as washing machine cartons to make houses, screens or shops.

6. Use builder's trays or grow bag trays for sand, small world play or dough. In this way you can provide for children who want to play independently.

7. Scarves, net curtains, fabric pieces and hats make dressing up more fun – provide some clothes pegs so children can fasten pieces independently to their own clothing.

8. Put a pop-up tent indoors for a quick role play area.

9. Use washing up bowls for water, sand, gloop or dry pasta.

10. Offer a basket with some puppets, a tea set and blanket, or a purse and money. Stand back and watch what happens.

Taking indoor activities outside.

Maintaining a balance between indoor and outdoor activity can be challenging. Strategies for combining and linking activities across both areas can help to lessen the gap for some children.

Twenty-one ways to bring the outdoors in and take the indoors out:

1. Put a plastic tunnel over the threshold and have entry and exit through the tunnel (children only!).

2. Put a pop-up tent just outside the door, joined to the tunnel over the threshold. This is good for wet days.

3. Leave a basket of playground chalk, a few whiteboards and pens, or a basket of clipboards to encourage writing and drawing outside.

4. Make up a picnic basket with a blanket, plates, cups, and so on, and leave it by the door so that children can set up house wherever they want.

5. Make a shop outside and encourage children to move between the inside and outside situations.

6. Put sign-making equipment in the technology area and encourage sign-making for outside games.

7. Have a post office inside and a parcel sorting room outside.

8. Get a length of hose with two funnels and talk through it through a window or other hole in the wall.

9. Spread a blanket or some carpet squares outside, and encourage children to play there with construction toys, books or puzzles.

10. Leave a basket or bowl on an inside table with a sign saying, 'Brown things in here please', or 'Red leaves today'.

11. Put a flipchart or easel outside for drawing or painting.

12. Leave some magnifying glasses out for close looking inside and out, along with paper and mark makers.

13. Encourage children to build railway lines, roads and constructions that link the inside and out.

14. Take some tables outside for reading or drawing.

15. Encourage children to feel free to take inside equipment outside.

16. Bring leaves, sticks and stones inside for children to look at.

17. Encourage children to use reference books to research birds, insects or animals.

18. Make shelters, homes, shops and dens inside as well as outside.

19. Make sure you have some boots and waterproof clothes so that children can go out every day.

20. Look outside every day – at the weather, the birds, or people passing.

21. Grow plants, seeds and bulbs indoors.

Children love to mimic their play on real life, which helps them to make sense of their world and process their experiences. Providing real items helps to make role play realistic and more fulfilling.

Real life items that promote high quality play:

- Mobile phones and cordless phones with the batteries removed
- Lengths of fabric, scarves, hats, caps and other real clothes for dressing up
- Real cutlery and crockery for domestic play
- Kitchen appliances with the wires and batteries removed
- Hole punchers, treasury tags and tape dispensers in the writing area
- Calculators for real maths
- Real tools (small size if possible) for gardening or woodwork
- Decorators' paintbrushes for painting with paint, water or paste
- Reflective safety waistcoats and hard hats
- Fine markers, ballpoints, highlighters and gel pens
- Clipboards for making notes and keeping scores
- Musical instruments
- Old-fashioned artefacts
- Pairs of glasses with the lenses removed, wigs, badges, overalls, purses, bags and cases
- Boxes, baskets and containers
- Small rucksacks and bags
- Post-it notes and stickers
- Forms, envelopes, junk mail, newspapers and magazines.

Many practitioners find themselves under pressure to cut back on the provision for high quality play experience for the young children in their care. The principles below should help you to remain committed to a child-centred early years curriculum.

Monitor your planning for play:

- Ensure that your agenda doesn't override the need for children to play and experience things first hand.
- Don't let the rush and hurry of the new curriculum squeeze out the need for time for high quality play.
- Don't let the demands of the new curriculum squeeze out the time for high quality play.
- Don't give in to 'top down' pressure from colleagues who do not understand the importance of play in the early years.

Step 3: **Maximizing learning through music**

Music constitutes a very important part of the early years curriculum. Generally, any music that is a 'good' example within its genre is suitable for use with young children. Just like adults, children enjoy hearing familiar pieces of music over and over again. This can be utilized so that music can be used at certain times of the day, such as to signal an activity, or to reassure and relax, or energize and excite children. Music can also be used to encourage discussion, to teach concepts and to create the right atmosphere for learning.

Learning through music page 102

It is useful to collect a 'library' or list of music, collecting a wide variety, such as opera, pop, film, classics, jazz, dance and world music. Many practitioners mark individual CDs with stickers noting the numbers of good tracks or keep a notebook in the box with the CDs and ask children to bring favourite music from home to add to the collection. It is illegal to copy these recordings, but borrowing CDs can enable you to make a 'wish list' of recordings to buy in the future. Collections such as the *Discover the Classics* volumes from Naxos can be a useful way to introduce music to your setting.

Careful preparation might help less musically experienced practitioners to avoid the mistake of this reception class teacher:

The first time I led an assembly I thought I had prepared everything down to the final detail. I was very nervous, as at that stage, the Year 1 and 2 children looked enormous to me! I had borrowed some CDs from the school collection and had selected what I thought was a really calm, soothing piece of music to play at the beginning and end of the assembly. Unfortunately, I didn't think to listen to the whole piece. Even more unfortunately, the Year 2 class was late arriving, so we were well into the track before they had all sat down.

That was when I discovered that the piece did not remain calm and soothing – it picked up tempo and became really energetic and rousing. By the time I was ready to begin the assembly, I had 80 children sitting in front of me ready to get up and boogie! I learned two lessons that day: one – that children are profoundly affected by the sound of music, and two – to always listen to a complete track before using it for a specific purpose. I can laugh about it now, but at the time I was mortified. Thankfully my colleagues were really nice about it and told me of their embarrassing mistakes as NQTs, which made me feel better!

A mother told the story of her son's introduction to classical music:

During my pregnancy I was working alone at home on a project that demanded total concentration. I found that if I worked to certain pieces of classical music such as Mozart, I could focus more fully on the task. I am by no means a music 'buff', but by the end of my pregnancy I was familiar with five or six CDs. My yoga teacher recommended that the women in our class used familiar music to help them to relax during childbirth, and so my son Aiden was born to the sound of Mozart.

His birth was peaceful and calm. I didn't think much about the music, until my husband put on a CD the next morning. I was holding Aiden and was amazed to see his head turn towards the music immediately. We later experimented by playing CDs that I had listened to regularly and some unfamiliar ones. Aiden definitely preferred the familiar tunes: they would calm him if he was upset, whereas the unfamiliar ones would have little effect. I realized that it was not only me who had been listening to Mozart for those nine months – I had helped develop my son's listening skills before he was even born!

General guidance

In their book *Music in the Early Years*, Susan Young and Joanne Glover give some guidance on choosing music as well as some tips for selecting and using music for young children.

Choosing music for young children:

- Children can listen to music of different lengths depending on familiarity and liking.
- Children are often open to music that adults could find challenging. They are not so 'set' in their ideas of what is/isn't music.
- Children often like music with a 'strong' element: a clear leading/solo instrument/voice; strong beat; gentle dynamics; or 'funny' sounds.
- Children shouldn't be expected to 'like' music because we think they should like it.
- Children shouldn't be expected to see or ascertain the composer's vision. This is sometimes expected with some commonly utilized music, for example *Peter and the Wolf*, *The Planets* or *Carnival of Animals*. However, they can be asked for their 'pictures' and learn of the composer's intentions.

Selecting and using music for young children:

- Choose music with a vivid timbre (a single voice, one, or two contrasting instruments) drawn from a range of times, places and cultures.
- Choose music with clear melodies and rhythms.
- If using short sections of a piece, fade it in at the beginning and out at the end so children know there is more of the piece. Young children can listen to and enjoy quite lengthy pieces if they know them well.

- Use a wide range of types of music. Use the music you like, but add some different types and be aware of what children hear at home and in the community.
- Children don't need pictures or stories to understand and enjoy music. 'They have no trouble in listening to music just as music.'

Listening to music gives the following opportunities:

- Getting to know the music
- Talking about individual responses to music
- Moving to music.

This will lead to:

- Careful listening, concentration and attention
- Following the music and noticing changes
- Remembering what is heard
- Responding to music in words, representations and music.[15]

Different types of music to use in the early years

Classical music
'Classical' is a word used generally to describe music composed in Europe, Australia and the Americas that is not folk or popular music although it may build on these traditions or borrow from them. From around the nineteenth century, music was more often composed to represent a story or picture. However, this sort of music should be used with care as a lot of orchestral music moves the melody around between parts, and young children can find it difficult to engage with it. Pieces with a strong element of rhythm or tune are a good way into classical music.

Pop music
Children usually like current pop music and are aware of 'pop idols' very early on, such as formula bands. They often know the words and some of the dance steps, which they can learn or show each other. Pop music with its repeated sections can develop movement and knowledge of words, and actions can be introduced by the teacher or leader. Some pop music of the past can also often prove popular, such as The Beach Boys or The Beatles.

Music from other cultures
Children respond well to music with a good beat, even if the rhythms are complex. They will enjoy moving, for instance, to Latin American music, African music, and music from Asia and the Caribbean, as well as fusion music – popular music that fuses with world music, such as *Afro Celt Sound System*.

Film music
Songs from films are often popular, and again offer the opportunity to learn words and create movements. An example would be using 'Let's Go Fly a Kite' from *Mary Poppins*, with children using ribbons to make shapes in the air. Films occasionally use music with 'classical' links, which can be a good way to introduce pieces of classical music. For example, 'If I had Words' from the film *Babe* is based on the final movement of 'Saint Saëns' *Concerto No. 3 for Organ*.

Fifteen times and places for using recorded music:

 First thing in the morning as children arrive

 As children gather on the carpet for group times

 Before time outdoors

 Just before lunch, for example to hear a piece which is becoming familiar

 Within a dance or music session, for moving bodies or hands, or for listening lying down

 On headphones in a listening corner

 During work sessions as background or stimulus

 At story time before, after or instead of a story

 As a stimulus for painting or drawing

 As background for role play

 As part of a listening session to stimulate imagination and discussion

 Outside, for quiet listening or to stimulate movement

 At clearing up time

 For early warning that the end of an activity or time period is approaching

 After lunch or an outdoor time to help refocus and quieten down.

Types of music for your collection:

- Quiet, lyrical music to relax the children, such as ballads, quiet classics or instrumentals

- Lively, jolly music to energize the children, such as marches, lively dance music or salsa

- Simple, easily recognized, short pieces of music to signal the start or end of an activity, such as TV and film themes, advertisement jingles, nursery rhymes and songs

- Music to demarcate the time needed for a task, such as short pieces of classics or film music

- Music to celebrate achievements, such as fanfares, circus music, opera or catchy pop songs

- Songs that teach certain skills, such as number or alphabet rhymes

- Music for adding actions, clapping, tapping and clicking fingers, such as jazz or lively dance or pop music.

Useful classics:

- *A Midsummer Night's Dream* – Mendelssohn
- *Cassation in G (Toy Symphony)* – attrib. Leopold Mozart
- 'Clog Dance' from *La Fille Mal Gardée* – Herold
- 'Fingal's Cave' from *The Hebrides Overture* – Mendelssohn
- *Mikrokosmos (extracts)* – Bartok
- *Norwegian Dance No. 2* – Grieg
- *Peer Gynt* – Grieg
- *The Little Train of the Caipira* – Villa-Lobos
- *The Nutcracker Suite* – Tchaikovsky
- *The Sorcerer's Apprentice* – Dukas

Step 4: Teaching and learning through movement

Brain Gym®
page 106

Young children need to interact with the world in a physical way and need plenty of opportunities for exploration and movement. There are physiological reasons for this. Aerobic movement increases the oxygen supply to the brain. Movement also reduces stress. There is also evidence that specific types of controlled, organized series of cross-lateral movements, called Brain Gym®, can help with learning by connecting both hemispheres of the brain and strengthening neural pathways.

Kishan is a strongly kinesthetic learner. He is lively and often boisterous, choosing frequently to engage in physical play outdoors. He shows more interest in activities that involve a practical approach than those that require a lot of looking or listening. For example, Kishan really enjoys 3D mind mapping, where he can gather artefacts, pictures and labels and physically manipulate them. This method of working suits him far better than making a mind map on paper or on a whiteboard. His teacher gives him plenty of opportunities for physical movement during each session. By building in movement and practical activities, she is catering to his natural learning style while also helping him to gradually develop better skills in visual and auditory learning.

A practitioner told a story about how she had to create more opportunities for physical movement when she took over a reception class:

I had always taught in Key Stage 2, but moved to teach Year 2 to fill in for a maternity leave. I thought it would be just for the short term, but I was surprised to find that I really enjoyed the younger children. When my headteacher asked me if I would be willing to take on Reception class the following September, I was excited, although somewhat apprehensive!

The first thing I learned was that, although I had provided for brain breaks and practical activities for my older classes, with these young children, I had to work from the basis of practical experience, then build in ways to verbalize and record their learning. The physical activity is the grounding of learning, not an 'add-on'. In a roundabout way, I realized that I should have been doing more practical activities with my older classes. If I return to Key Stage 2, that is a lesson that I will take with me.

Twelve brain break activities:

1. Helicopter spin (*gets the fluid in the inner ear moving*)
   Stand in a space with arms outstretched. Spin in one direction, to a count of ten. Spin in the opposite direction, to a count of ten.

2. The owl (*cross-lateral movement that releases stress and improves hand-eye co-ordination; particularly good for during fine motor activities*)
   Cross one arm to put hand on opposite shoulder and squeeze. Turn head in the direction of the same shoulder. Take a deep breath and pull shoulders back. Turn head to look over other shoulder, keeping chin level and tracking with eyes. Turn head back to centre. Drop head to chest and take a deep breath, making a 'whoo-oo' when breathing out. Repeat with other arm and shoulder.

3. Miss a word (*develops 'inner speech' and helps comprehension and reading skills*)
   Choose any familiar song with repetition, such as 'Row, Row, Row the Boat', and explain to the children that you are going to practise singing the song inside and outside their heads. Choose a word that is to be sung inside their head, such as 'merrily'. Sing the song through once with all the words. Sing the song with the chosen word missed. Sing the whole song again.

4. Body blither (*good brain break or energizer*)
   Vigorously wiggle the hands. Add the shoulders, arms, hips, legs and feet. Accompany with the sound that is made when cheeks and lips are relaxed and shaken.

5. The voice (*stimulates and increases oxygen to the brain; good preparation for concentration*)
    Stand in a circle. Give three loud sighs using the 'ah' sound and breathing out on each. Pick a mid-range tone and sustain this using 'ah' for a count of ten. Switch to a high pitch and the 'ee' sound for a count of ten (breathing where necessary!). Switch to a low sound and 'oooo' for a count of ten. Now let the children choose the sound and the pitch, freely moving from pitch to pitch and sound to sound for a count of 20. Gradually increase the time for each part of the exercise.

6. Fire engines (*good brain break or energizer*)
    Sing 'ah' with the voice as low as it can go. Sweep it up to as high as it can go. Sweep down again. Repeat four or five times.

7. Lazy eights (*co-ordinates both eyes, improves balance and co-ordination*)
    Reach out with one hand and draw a big '8' on its side, starting in front of the nose. Draw the same kind of '8' with the other hand, making it as large as possible. Follow the hand with the eyes. Repeat each one four or five times.

8. The swing (*loosens muscles after sitting, improves balance and co-ordination, increases breathing rate*)
    Stand up and relax knees slightly. Let the head and shoulders hang forward. Swing slowly to the left and right like a pendulum. Repeat up to five times, then slowly uncurl back to standing. Try this standing with legs crossed at the ankles for children with good balance.

9. Bee's knees (*cross-lateral activity*)
    Stand with legs slightly bent and apart. Put hands on knees. Move knees together and as they touch, change hands to opposite knees. Move back as knees come apart. Repeat several times.

10. Rub your tummy (*concentration and focus*)
    Stand up. Rub tummy with one hand, pat head with other. Continue for a count of 20. Change hands and repeat.

11. Secret shapes (*sensory learning, concentration, fine motor skills*)
    In pairs: one child draws on the other child's back (a shape, letter or picture). The partner guesses what it is. Swap and repeat.

12. Finger fun (*fine motor control, hand-eye movement*)
    Make a steeple with the fingers in front of the face. Lift each pair of fingers apart in turn.

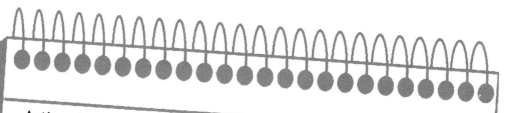

Action rhymes and songs that can be used for brain breaks:

- Heads, shoulders, knees and toes
- In a cottage in a wood
- Two fat gentlemen
- Down in the jungle
- There was a princess long ago
- The farmer's in his den
- In and out the dusty bluebells
- Here we go round the mulberry bush
- Ring-a-roses
- One finger, one thumb keep moving
- This old man, he played one
- I am the music man
- Two little dickey birds
- The wheels on the bus
- If you're happy and you know it
- Teddy bear, teddy bear, touch your nose
- 1, 2, 3, 4, 5, once I caught a fish alive
- Five little monkeys
- When Goldilocks went to the house of the bears
- Miss Polly had a dolly
- Wind the bobbin up
- Twinkle, twinkle, little star

Step 5: The place for technology

Technology page 108

There are many applications of technology that are appropriate for the early years, in addition to computers and high-tech equipment. Authors and researchers such as Jane Healy give guidance about how to monitor the use of technology and ensure that it is used to encourage good learning behaviours. Children need to become competent in using a wide variety of types of technology, while also developing the essential skills that enable them to operate independently of it when appropriate. This can be done through the seizing of everyday opportunities to use technology, such as simply letting children switch on the dishwasher or teaching them to use a stopwatch to time themselves riding the bikes, in addition to a more structured approach towards computer use.

One pre-school leader described how she was concerned that her group of children did not have access to a computer and worried that the children in her care were missing out on an important aspect of their early education:

When prospective parents came to visit, they would invariably ask about computers. Whereas the nursery school down the road has an impressive array of technology, we are still somewhat limited, mainly due to funds, but also due to the lack of storage and security for such expensive equipment.

I was always acutely aware that we simply don't measure up to what is provided in many other settings. Then one day, a family visited with their three-year-old son. The dad told me that he was a computer engineer, so I waited for the inevitable question about our provision for technology, but it didn't come. This puzzled me, and when the family were about to leave, I commented that he hadn't asked me about technology and computers.

He looked at me in surprise and said that technology involves far more than computers. He pointed out some ways that he had seen children using technology during their visit: the children who were using the tape recorder and headphones to listen to stories in the book area; the cookery group who helped to set the timer on the oven; and the child who switched on the music at clearing-up time. After this, I made a list of ways that the children in our group used technology on a regular basis, and included it in our pack of information for new parents.

Groups from George's pre-school sometimes visit the nursery class in the school, where they use the roamer turtle and simple paint programs on the computer. This is a new and unfamiliar experience for George, whose family does not own a computer. However, George's friend Jo has been using her mum's computer in a wide variety of ways since she was very young, and can independently produce pictures, edit and print them. The pre-school practitioners are careful to monitor the pairings of children who work together because of this wide range of skills within the group. George learns from Jo's lead, and Jo listens to their key-worker, who suggests that she shows George what to do rather than taking control of the activity.

This method of allowing one child to teach another has been proved to be highly effective and is used extensively by the pre-school staff. However, they were still surprised by George's actions when one day the CD player would not work. George took the remote control from his key-worker, removed the back and took out the batteries. He then asked for new batteries, which he carefully installed in the correct positions, while explaining what he was doing to his key-worker. He pressed 'Play', and the music started. George clearly had knowledge and skills in technology that his friend Jo, and even some of the practitioners, possibly lacked!

Fascinating Facts

● Before the age of five, children cannot separate fact from fiction, for example in television viewing. By the age of seven, most children have begun to understand the difference between appearance and reality. However, this development is inversely related to the child's exposure to television – the more he watches, the less well he can discriminate. Some children still believe that the computer is 'alive' at the age of eight or nine![16]

● A recent study into children as consumers showed that until they are at least eight years old, children do not understand the difference between adverts and normal television broadcasting. Researcher Dr Caroline Oates from the University of Sheffield reported to the British Psychological Society in 2002 that until the age of eight or even ten, children rarely understand the intention of adverts. Before the age of eight, many children think that advertisements are shown not only to give viewers a break, but also to give the characters on the television a rest![17]

Twenty-four ways to introduce children to ICT without the use of a computer:

1. Teach children to help you to set clocks and alarms for timed activities.

2. Provide simple tape recorders and teach children to use them independently.

3. Allow children to use the telephone under supervision.

4. Allow children to help to set the microwave, dishwasher or washing machine.

5. Create a balance in cookery sessions between making things by hand and using modern appliances.

6. Provide equipment for role play in the home corner, such as telephones, mobile phones with the batteries removed or remote controls.

7. Allow children to play with pieces of equipment, for example disconnected keyboards from old computers, hairdryers and toasters with the plugs and wires removed.

8. Help children to take apart and fit together old pieces of equipment such as radios or cassette recorders.

9. Borrow a karaoke machine and let the children have fun using it.

10. Point out the use of technology in everyday situation such as the weighing scales or scanning equipment at the supermarket.

11. Provide toys such as remote control cars for occasional play sessions.

12. Ask children to help you to set the timer on the video recorder.

The telephone is a simple way to use ICT.

Use electronic scales to practise other forms of ICT.

13. Allow children to take photographs or help with a video camera on important occasions.

14. Involve children in real life situations where you use a calculator and talk through and explain what you are doing.

15. Provide calculators for children to use in play situations, for example when playing 'shop'.

16. Encourage children to help with everyday tasks, such as using a remote control to switch on the music for tidy-up time.

17. Go on a technology walk to see what you can find, such as street lights, cameras, automatic doors, checkout tills, parking meters, cash machines, telephones, satellite dishes and petrol pumps.

18. Use a watch with an alarm to time activities.

19. Use an overhead projector to project pictures on walls and screens.

20. When you buy new role play equipment select up-to-date models, even if they don't really work, such as hands-free or cordless phones rather than ones with wires, and microwaves in addition to traditional ovens.

21. Use electronic bathroom scales to weigh people, teddies and toys.

22. Explore Teletext on the TV and the different ways to use remote controls.

23. Use a digital camera to make books and sequences of pictures of recent experiences.

24. Make a scrapbook of equipment that has digital displays or buttons. Use junk mail and free catalogues to find pictures.

Guidelines for pre-schoolers who use computers

If you have access to computers and the policy in your setting is to use them, these guidelines from Jane Healy's book[18], are a useful basis for monitoring their use.

- Starting children on computers too early is far worse than starting them too late.
- A child should be able to understand the cause–effect relationship of moving a mouse or touching the screen to get a reaction before she starts to use a computer.
- Look for software that makes the child feel independent.
- Downplay skill-and-drill maths and phonics activities in favour of interactive problem solving or more open-ended uses.
- Discourage impulsive clicking. Stop the program occasionally to encourage the child to talk about what is happening, what he is doing and why.
- Supplement 'eyes-on' with 'hands-on'. Find real life experiences that extend and complement the virtual ones.
- Help the child understand how the computer works and what's going on as he manipulates a program. Let him see how you physically connect computer, printer and other components. Keep emphasizing that people control the computer, not the other way around.
- Don't let screen time substitute for lap time and don't expect books on CD-ROM to substitute for interactive reading with loving adults.
- Consider eliminating the use of clip art if you decide to let your child use digital drawing tools.
- Evaluate the aesthetic qualities of software, including, of course, CD-ROMS.
- If your child goes on the internet, closely supervise him.
- Whenever possible, make computer use a social experience by putting two chairs at the machine and encouraging conversation and collaboration with peers, siblings or adults.
- If your young child begins to show signs of computer addiction, cut down on or eliminate screen time and make sure plenty of alternative activities are available.
- Don't ever forget that the best multimedia, interactive environment is the real world.

Make computer use a social experience whenever possible.

Twenty-one questions to ask when evaluating the use of computers in your setting:

1. Are all programs evaluated before use?

2. Do the programs actually develop the skills claimed by the producers, or are they 'empty of real learning'?

3. Do the programs move too fast or too slowly?

4. Are the children encouraged to think before answering?

5. What happens if a child responds impulsively?

6. How are thoughtful responses rewarded?

7. How would children know if their responses were appropriate?

8. Could a child be rewarded for repeatedly guessing?

9. Do the programs encourage independent use by children?

10. Do the adults spend time getting to know the programs before the children use them?

11. Do all the adults have the necessary skills to help children with ICT?

12. Do we promote ICT as a positive, exciting tool or a frightening 'male' thing?

13. Are the chairs for children and adults the right height? (Children should be able to sit with their feet on the floor, looking straight ahead at the screen.)

14. Do the computers have enough memory to run the programs without crashing or working so slowly that children become frustrated?

15. Are the mouse mats big enough?

16. Have we considered the use of alternatives such as track balls and larger 'mice' for small hands?

17. Have we looked for programs that are interactive and thought provoking?

18. Have we taught children how to adjust the volume of the music and speech so they can hear but not disturb others?

19. Do we offer children headphones to use with the computer to enable them to concentrate?

20. Do we ask children to feed back at group and plenary times, giving ICT status in discussion?

21. Have we shown the children a simple way of recording time spent on ICT, such as tick charts, signing up boards or Velcro® labels?

Part Four

Teaching for intelligence

Step 1: Creative teaching for better learning

One of the most effective ways to challenge children's thinking and enrich learning is to provide unusual, exciting activities. When the unexpected happens, children need to draw on past experiences to make sense of the new. They need to reconsider their current understanding of the concept and check it against new criteria, often leading to a new level of understanding. The importance of active learning is far greater than simply its influence upon levels of academic attainment. Active learning also positively affects children's emotional and moral development. It has been shown that the actual process of learning is as important as the learning outcome. By thinking creatively, practitioners provide a stimulating and exciting environment that is best suited to the natural brain development of young children.

Better learning page 111

As Carrie plays with the cornflour and water mixture, she talks quietly under her breath, 'Oooh, it's all ucky, ucky, ucky! Oh, sticky – ugh! Aaah, now it's – ha, ha, (laughs), it's soggy now!' Her teacher plays in the tray next to her. 'Oh, ugh! It's quite hard in the tray,' she says to herself, 'I have to scrape it up with my fingernails. Oh, but when I hold it up, it gets runny – it's turned into a liquid!' After a few minutes, Carrie starts to use the word 'runny' in her description. She does not pick up on the word 'liquid' but her teacher makes a mental note to introduce that word again in the future with her group.

When contractors arrived one morning to work on the school grounds, the children in the nursery were really interested in what they were doing. They spent long periods of time hanging on the fence talking about the diggers and machines.

The next day, the practitioners made a pile of sand on the nursery playground. Next to it, they put various toy trucks, diggers, shovels and buckets, along with clipboards, pens, tape measures and rulers. The children immediately started working with the sand, measuring, shovelling and moving it from place to place. Soon they started constructing with the bricks, and two children fetched cones to block off areas of danger.

At the end of the session, the group spent 20 minutes sweeping the sand and tidying it back into the sandpit for the next day, when construction work started again.

Forty ways to get creative:

1. Put sponges in the sand tray.
2. Put coloured fish tank gravel at the bottom of the water tray.
3. Tie lengths of cardboard tubing around the room and provide a big bag of balls to roll down them.
4. Put food colouring in ice cubes and use for play in plastic bowls or the water tray.
5. Put out 'bath crayons' with the water tray.
6. Fill trays with wet, oozy mud from the garden.
7. Put out a variety of paper towels and tissues beside the water tray.
8. Mix cornflour in shallow trays with a small amount of water and food colourings and let children enjoy it oozing through their fingers.
9. Lay out seeds, pots and compost for planting – but add some pasta shells, plastic buttons, wooden beads, marbles and other items that will not grow.
10. Blow bubbles outside or inside.
11. Hang or pin notes and messages on doors, branches, on chairs or in sheds.
12. Leave a piece of special material such as velvet, sequinned fabric or bright satin for children to discover.
13. Freeze water in wellington boots, rubber gloves and other interesting containers, and then float them in the water tray.
14. Leave something in an unusual place – a teddy in the bathroom, a single shoe in the reading corner, a fireman's hat in the garden. Ask the children why they think it is there.
15. Use spray bottles or paintbrushes with water or weak paint on huge pieces of paper pinned to walls or fences.
16. Make a wormery or an ant farm. Send for a butterfly box so you can watch the caterpillars grow.

Challenge children's thinking by supplying unusual materials.

17. Leave a small backpack on the outside door handle. Add items such as a pair of binoculars, a disposable camera, a compass or a clipboard to spark imaginative play.

18. Leave a nest of gold-sprayed eggs (hard boiled) in a corner of the garden.

19. Take time to watch things, such as fish in a tank, ants on the playground, shadows or clouds.

20. Go on listening, smelling or shape walks.

21. Give children carbon paper to experiment with. It emphasizes the permanence of marks and is an old technology that can provide hours of exploration and fun.

22. Have a treasure hunt with picture clues.

23. Write letters to a real or imaginary person.

24. Make a postbox.

25. Watch a puddle evaporate.

26. Bring in some flowers, an unusual plant or some seeds, and leave them on a table.

27. Bring in some unusual fruits or vegetables and let children help to cut them up and look at what is inside.

28. Fetch unusual things from recycling centres. Don't worry if you can't think of a use for them – the children will, and this is part of the fun!

29. Make a dragon from a cardboard box. Tell the children that he wants to talk to them – but he is rather deaf, so they have to write him notes and feed them to him.

30. Combine unexpected things – string in the water tray, stones buried in the sand.

31. Ask the children to help you rearrange an area of the room or the whole room. Draw plans and discuss how you should do it.

32. Hang sound-makers in bushes and on fences.

33. Draw arrows or lines on the floor or outside.

34. Plan an outing with the children. Make lists and preparations, timelines, letters or invitations.

35. Put a message in a bottle.

36. Make a sandwich with a strange filling such as sequins, grass or plastic spiders, and then talk about who it might be for.

37. Bring a small suitcase packed for a story book character's holiday.

38. Bury things in the garden and let the children dig them up, such as old coins, shells or shiny marbles.

39. Sort out a button box.

40. Put things in a feely bag, such as dough or gloop (a mixture of cornflour and water to make consistency gloopy) in a plastic bag, feathers, a lumpy or spiky seed, or some fur fabric.

Children need little encouragement to go on an adventure!

Twenty-five items to collect for creative teaching:

1. Boxes and containers of all sizes and shapes
2. Baskets and bowls
3. Bags of all sizes and shapes
4. A feely bag or box
5. Beads, buttons and badges
6. Ribbon, tape and coloured string
7. Wrapping paper, gift tags and cards, gift ribbon
8. Stickers of all sizes and shapes
9. Food colouring
10. Junk mail, catalogues and phone books
11. Empty envelopes (used or new)
12. Books, papers and leaflets in other languages
13. Tickets and labels
14. Foreign coins
15. Menus and guidebooks
16. Shiny card and paper for badges and labels
17. Small whiteboards and clipboards
18. Clothes pegs
19. Zip-lock bags
20. Magnifying glasses
21. Felt pens from thin to mega thick
22. Feathers, shells and shiny stones
23. Puppets (finger, hand and bigger)
24. Pieces of interesting fabrics
25. A flip chart to use inside and out.

Fifteen 'What would happen if?' questions:

 What would happen if we put the cardboard tubes in the water tray?

 What would happen if we cut the fruit sideways instead of downwards?

 What would happen if we hung the wet tea towels out on an icy day?

 What would happen if we left something out all night?

 What would happen if we moved this piece of furniture?

 What would happen if we wrote a letter to ourselves and posted it?

 What would happen if we left one of the ingredients out of a recipe?

 What would happen if we put some nesting material in the garden in spring?

 What would happen if we put some bird food out?

 What would happen if we put food colouring in the water?

 What would happen if we painted in the rain?

 What would happen if we put leaves or grass in the freezer?

 What would happen if we wrote to the Queen or the Prime Minister?

 What would happen if we mixed sequins in the sand?

 What would happen if we could write backwards?

Step 2: **Fostering the beginnings of group-work**

The importance of fostering good group-work skills is now seen as an important aspect of early years education. Co-operation in groups leads to better quality language and interactions. During the foundation stage, there is naturally a mixture of time spent in different types of groups. The balance of time spent in different types of groups will largely depend on the aims of the practitioner, who needs to bear in mind the fact that each child will be at some stage on the continuum between playing alone and working confidently in a group. The practitioner needs to organize activities that help children to develop the social skills that group-work demands, at whatever stage of development they have reached.

Group-work page 114

When George went through a phase of playing alongside one particular boy in the sand tray for long periods every morning, his key-worker decided to encourage the boys to interact more by altering the equipment that was provided. She set up the tray one morning with just one very large sand wheel and a selection of spades, moving the buckets to another shelf where the children would have had to actively seek them out if they had wanted them. At first, George and his friend both wanted the sand wheel to themselves, and a gentle tussle took place. Neither boy could pour any sand in and make it spin, because they were too busy trying to dominate the wheel! The key-worker stepped in and took a spade herself. She stood the wheel back up and started to pour sand in. The wheel spun and both boys were excited. 'Hey, if you two help, we'll be able to get it going faster,' she suggested. George and his friend started to shovel sand into the top of the wheel. After a few minutes the key-worker withdrew, leaving the children playing together.

Activity: monitoring group-work

Either when planning or when reviewing the week's activities, use the checklist below to monitor the variety of group-work that children will experience. The aim should be that all the different sorts of groupings should be used during the week. Children should work in all sorts of groups and combinations, some self selected, some directed.

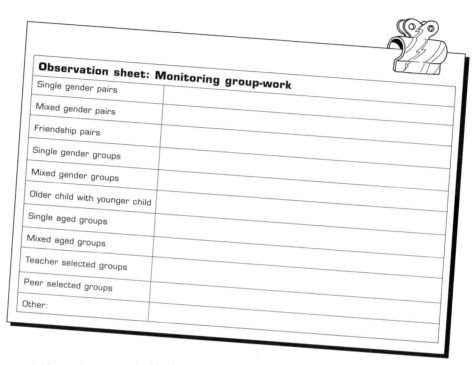

Observation sheet: Monitoring group-work

Single gender pairs	
Mixed gender pairs	
Friendship pairs	
Single gender groups	
Mixed gender groups	
Older child with younger child	
Single aged groups	
Mixed aged groups	
Teacher selected groups	
Peer selected groups	
Other:	

For full-size photocopiable version, see end of book.

Children love jobs such as unpacking the shopping.

Thirty-five practical jobs for children:

1. Watering the indoor and outdoor plants
2. Sweeping up the floor at the end of the day
3. Preparing snack food, cutting and peeling fruit, counting out biscuits and cups
4. Pouring drinks at snack time
5. Washing up after cookery sessions or snacks
6. Cleaning the pets' cages or fish tanks
7. Handing out notes to parents at the end of the day
8. Mixing paint for the art area
9. Washing paint pots and brushes
10. Tightening bolts on equipment such as tricycles when they work loose
11. Packing the dishwasher and putting it on
12. Unpacking the shopping after a trip to the supermarket
13. Washing and sorting maths equipment
14. Reorganizing the role play area and choosing a new theme
15. Washing the dolls and dolls clothes from the home corner
16. Weeding or sweeping up leaves in the garden
17. Putting up displays – they will soon learn how to do this, if helped
18. Collecting and putting away outdoor apparatus and toys
19. Cleaning whiteboards and putting them away
20. Putting out chairs, mats or cushions for group time
21. Writing shopping and To Do lists
22. Helping to assemble new pieces of equipment
23. Organizing and reorganizing equipment on shelves
24. Making labels and notices
25. Feeding the pets
26. Putting wellington boots in pairs and clipping them with pegs
27. Using a small bell to signal that it's time to pack up, go to assembly or have snacks
28. Filling water trays and bowls
29. Wiping down tables at the end of the session
30. Helping to carry boxes of equipment to the cupboards at the end of the session
31. Helping to choose new equipment for the setting
32. Filling planters with soil
33. Planting things such as cress, bulbs, cuttings and plants
34. Sweeping up puddles after rain
35. Sprinkling salt on frosty paths.

Twenty ways to organize groups:

1. By first names beginning with certain letters of the alphabet

2. By surnames beginning with certain letters of the alphabet

3. By alphabetical order

4. By register order

5. By the types of shoes that the children are wearing

6. By the months of children's birthdays

7. By pets: who has a dog, a cat, a hamster, or no pets

8. By who has brothers, sisters, both, or no siblings

9. By where the children live

10. By clothing, such as tights, dungarees, cardigans or sweatshirts

11. By how the children travelled to school

12. By favourite colours

13. By what the children ate for breakfast

14. By eye colour

15. By curly, straight, long or short hair

16. By what activity the children did that morning

17. By what the children chose to eat at snack time

18. By asking them a question

19. By passing a soft toy round with a song playing – whoever is holding the toy each time the music stops, joins each group in turn

20. By tapping the children on the head and counting to ten – the tenth child joins each group in turn.

The High/Scope model of 'Plan – Work – Recall'

The High/Scope model of 'Plan – Work – Recall' is familiar to many practitioners, while others may be familiar with the similar model of 'Plan – Do – Review'.[19]

Plan

Each child decides what they will do during the period and shares this with an adult in a small group. The plan is recorded in some way, either by the practitioner or the child, or both together. The purpose is to connect children's interests with purposeful actions.

Work

The children begin their chosen activities and continue until they have completed their plans or changed them. As the children work, the adults move among them, watching closely and supporting them if they need or request it. This part of the session usually lasts from 45 to 55 minutes. Then children clear up and store unfinished projects.

Recall

Children meet with their adult to share what they have done. Adults question and discuss the activities. The purpose is to help children to reflect on, understand and build on their actions.

Step 3: Teaching through VAK

A simple model for understanding individual learning styles is to break them down into three categories: *visual*, *auditory* and *kinesthetic*. These equate to: *seeing*, *hearing* and *doing*. Everybody has a preferred style, but will also utilize all three methods. These preferences may be strong in some children, meaning that the practitioner has to work hard to ensure that a balance is found where there is an equal demand upon children's visual, auditory and kinesthetic engagement. She also needs to monitor the timetable to ensure that there is a VAK balance. A simple way to do this is to include a box with the letters 'V', 'A' and 'K' next to each activity on your planning sheet. If you have too many ticks in any one area, you will know to reconsider your planning.

VAK learning page 116

Carrie's mother is often asked how she 'taught' Carrie to recognize her letters and read some words. Her mother is puzzled, because Carrie effectively taught herself. But she read to Carrie from the age of four or five months, she takes her to the library every week, she talks about words and signs as they go about their daily routine, and she provides toys and plays games that encourage visual learning.

Carrie also had a set of foam letters that she plays with in the bath, building blocks with letters and numbers on them and an alphabet puzzle. When engaged in play with these toys, her mother adds information about the letters and numbers as she talks, along with information about colours and shapes: 'Oh, you're putting the blue brick on top of the yellow one – uh-oh! Will it balance?' 'Yep, I think so, anyway, it might do, it might not go crash,' Carrie says, and her mother comments, 'You're right! Well done! You've balanced the blue letter "D" on top of the yellow letter "J"!'

For Carrie's mother this was an instinctive part of the way that she communicated with her child. She did not consider herself to be 'teaching' Carrie, but if we analyse what information she was giving in just that short interaction, we can see the potential for Carrie's learning. She identified the colours of the bricks, along with the positioning of the blue one 'on top' of the yellow one. She used the word 'balance' and asked Carrie a question about what she thought the outcome would be as she put the final brick on the top. She then responded to Carrie's reply and drew her attention to the letters on the bricks that Carrie had balanced, along with repeating the names of the colours.

A nursery teacher was frustrated by the fidgeting that went on during every story time. It seemed that she could never finish a story because she was constantly having to stop to ask children to let go of one another's clothing or to stop playing with the Velcro® fastenings on their shoes! She asked a colleague to observe a story time to give an insight into what was happening. She was surprised when her colleague told her that the fidgeting always started with the same two children, then 'spread' outwards until the whole group was more interested in their shoe fastenings than the story!

The colleague suggested giving the children, particularly these two active ones, something more physical to do during story time, such as using more props or involving children in lifting the flaps of the book or doing actions to go with the stories. She also suggested that she could sometimes offer the children beany toys or teddies to hold at story time so they had something to do with their hands and were less likely to disturb others.

Thirty ways to exploit visual learning:

1. Display mind maps for a variety of topics and concepts.

2. Take photographs of activities for group discussions and reflection.

3. Label everyday items around the room.

4. Play lots of visual memory games such as 'Snap' and 'Pairs' with flashcards and 'flash pictures'.

5. Use small world toys, puppets or soft toys as props when you tell stories.

6. Use visual cues for labelling places and belongings.

7. Draw maps and plans of journeys and places.

8. Encourage children to add pictures and captions to mind maps.

9. Draw attention to patterns in everyday experiences and give children the chance to copy and repeat them.

10. Make displays and books of photographs of previous experiences.

11. Use pictures and photographs of classroom materials for labelling and organizational purposes.

12. Make posters that demonstrate what has been learned, for example a poster with lots of coloured triangles or squares.

13. Provide a wealth of books and reading resources.

14. Encourage children to play matching games.

15. Go on 'spotting' walks to look for shapes, letters, colours or patterns.

16. Use visual recall to help with mapping out memories of experiences, such as, 'What did you see at the fair?' or 'What did the animals at the zoo look like?'

17. Encourage children to draw pictures of the things they make, or of events and activities. Encourage different ways of recording, such as labelled diagrams, pictures, comic strips or making little books with no words.

18. Use mirrors to help children look for detail when they draw themselves or things in the setting.

19. Encourage children to play with jigsaw and other pictorial puzzles.

20. Use close-up photographs or partially covered pictures for games, such as guessing the object from a picture showing just a detail or a part of the object.

21. Play 'I spy with my little eye', adapting the game to use categories such as, 'Something with stripes', 'Something round and blue' or 'Something with a silver top'.

22. Play 'Guess the person'. Describe a person in the room in detail, encouraging the children to look at each other carefully.

23. Put some objects on a tray, cover them with a cloth, remove the cloth for a short time, cover it again and see who can remember all the objects.

24. Next, show the objects, then ask the children to shut their eyes while you remove one, and see who can tell which object is missing.

25. Label children's coat pegs, snack plates, water bottles, drawers or lockers. Use just a picture to start with, then a picture with the child's initial, then a picture and the name, then just the name.

26. Play 'Spot the difference' each day as the children arrive. Remove or move one or two things, and see if they can spot what has moved. Start with big, obvious things!

27. Play 'Spot the difference', but asking the children to notice what is new. Add an item such as a vase of flowers, an unusual fruit in the fruit bowl or a new picture on the wall each day.

28. Make visual links with the stories and events that children experience, such as coloured checks on wrapping paper with Elmer stories, a flower with a walk to the park, or a packet of porridge with *The Three Bears*.

29. Use story sacks to help children to visualize stories.

30. Wear something significant that is linked to the theme of the day or week, such as red socks, scarf and cap if you are learning about colours, or a floppy hat and big sunglasses if your theme is 'Summer'.

Visual skills can be encouraged by the use of mirrors.

Thirty ways to exploit auditory learning:

1. Encourage children to pole-bridge.

2. Work alongside children, talking about what you are doing.

3. Allow plenty of time for review sessions.

4. Review mind maps verbally.

5. Give opportunities for learning through music.

6. Go on listening walks in the garden or around your setting.

7. Use tapes of stories and songs alongside books.

8. Use different voices when you read stories and poems.

9. Ask children to talk through their plans before embarking on an activity.

10. Ask children to talk about what they are doing at various stages of a task.

11. Demonstrate new skills while explaining clearly what you are doing.

12. Talk through mind maps while you make them.

13. Encourage children to put new vocabulary and concepts to music.

14. Make up short 'raps' about activities and what has been learned.

15. Use 'each one teach one' where each child talks to a friend about what he has discovered.

16. Record children talking, singing or reading, and then play the tapes back and guess 'Who is this?'

17. Allow children plenty of time to discuss what they plan to do either with an adult or another child.

18. Pause during stories and group discussions to enable children to talk in pairs about what has happened and predict what comes next.

19. Use pre-recorded listening tapes or CDs to play games such as, 'Sound lotto', 'Spot the animal', 'Whose baby is this?', 'What is the street sound?' or 'Guess which instrument is playing'.

20. Encourage children to make sounds and music to accompany stories, either with you or in small groups to perform to others.

21. Use music sessions to develop skills such as listening, turn-taking and sound patterns.

22. Use puppets and soft toys to help establish characters and different voices.

23. Use recall of sound to help with mapping out memories of experiences, such as, 'What did you hear at the fair?' or 'What did the animals at the zoo sound like?'

24. Use instruments or body sounds to play a version of 'Simon says' where you clap or stamp or play a rhythm, and the children copy.

25. Sing songs with a strong rhythmic beat.

26. Clap, click or make another small noise as you count or spell.

27. Talk through letter and number formation as you draw in the air, such as 'Round the ball and down the stick'.

28. Sound out letters as you spell or write them.

29. Use music to re-create or establish a mood or event.

30. Use music or a sound, such as a little bell, chime bar or squeaker to indicate snack time or clearing-up time.

Auditory skills are practised on a listening walk.

Thirty ways to exploit kinesthetic learning:

1. Encourage children to manipulate pictures and objects for 3D mind maps.

2. Build 3D practical aspects into your displays.

3. Incorporate movement and actions into story-telling sessions.

4. Practise fine motor skills such as handwriting through large motor activity.

5. Act out stories. If you can get the hall or another big space, use it!

6. Have story or discussion time outside so that children can move and spread out.

7. Encourage children to help to move and rearrange the outside apparatus regularly.

8. In the winter, bring some of the big blocks inside.

9. Provide plenty of opportunity for role play.

10. Include lots of practical music-making in music sessions.

11. Encourage children to make big, extravagant gestures as they tell stories or talk about their play.

12. Give children opportunities to play with and manipulate wooden, foam or magnetic letters and numerals.

13. Encourage children to draw letters and numbers in the air, in sand, on the whiteboard or in finger paints.

14. Teach new playground games and incorporate new concepts into the physical activity.

15. Use recall of movement to help with mapping out memories of experiences, such as 'What did you do at the fair?' or 'How did the animals at the zoo move?'

16. Use fabrics and other textures to help children to recall experiences.

17. Make or buy a feely bag and use it to explore in three dimensions.

18. Make lots of big, extravagant gestures as you explain an activity or tell a story.

19. Make sure the outside toys and apparatus have multiple uses. Guttering and pipes, ropes, tyres, boxes and crates give far more scope for play than fixed apparatus.

20. Provide plenty of manipulative toys, things with moving parts and construction toys, both large and small.

21. In music sessions, make sure that there is plenty of movement. Accompany movement with sound, make movement in response to sounds and practise stopping and starting, changing speed and moving in patterns.

22. Provide plenty of malleable materials such as clay, dough, slime, pasta, bubbles, sand, water and finger paints. Try as many of these activities as you can out of doors, with bigger paper, bigger quantities and bigger movements.

23. Offer playground chalk, or paint and big brushes, to make tracks and roads on the path outside.

24. Include children in lots of physical gardening activities.

25. Include tunnels, bridges, balance bars, stepping stones, and cones in your play equipment.

26. In the winter, try to give children opportunities to use this apparatus in the hall or another big space if you can't get outside.

27. Provide blankets, rope and pegs and encourage the children to build camps outside or, if the weather is inclement, clear space for them to do it indoors.

28. Make opportunities for children to read and write in role play activities, such as clipboards and whiteboards to use indoors and out, message pads, parking tickets, score pads, telephone books and menus.

29. Provide plenty of equipment for fine motor control, such as bead threading, lacing and sewing cards, marble rolls, sorting and counting apparatus.

30. Encourage children to use their hands and fingers to count, draw and write.

Writing in the air particularly benefits kinesthetic learners.

Step 4: Engaging the multiple intelligences

To my mind, a human intellectual competence must entail a set of skills of problem solving – enabling the individual to resolve genuine problems or difficulties that he or she encounters and, when appropriate, to create an effective product – and must also entail the potential for finding or creating problems – thereby laying the groundwork for new knowledge.

Howard Gardner[4]

Eight intelligences page 122

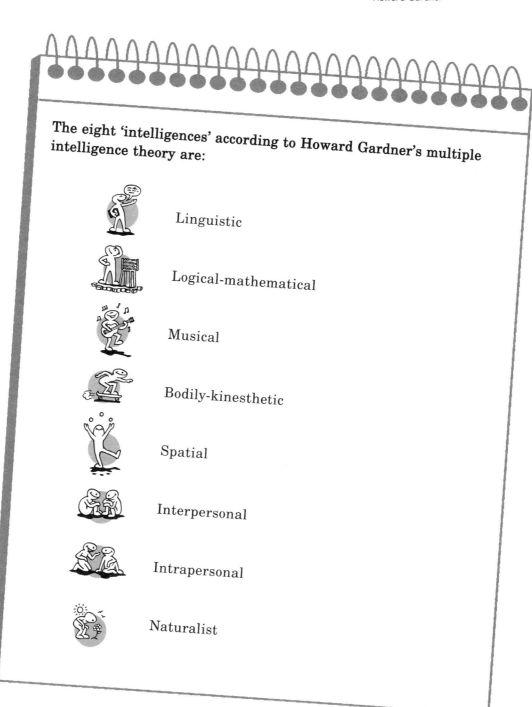

The eight 'intelligences' according to Howard Gardner's multiple intelligence theory are:

Linguistic

Logical-mathematical

Musical

Bodily-kinesthetic

Spatial

Interpersonal

Intrapersonal

Naturalist

Each individual child has a combination of different intelligences in different strengths, and the early years environment will influence how these different intelligences develop and flourish. As with seeking a VAK balance, the practitioner needs to monitor the activities in order to give equal emphasis to the different forms of intelligence and ways of learning. A checklist with the initials for the multiple intelligences can be used when planning to monitor those that are covered within a session, and those that might need more emphasis at a later stage.

Each of our four children has particular strengths in several areas and different ability levels in the others. Samantha clearly has a strong linguistic intelligence, but she also has a strong musical intelligence. She has a good sense of rhythm and pitch and can recall a simple pattern and tune after hearing it just once. George, on the other hand, has a leaning towards the naturalist intelligence. He is very interested in nature and notices details about the natural world. For example, he once collected a bucket full of snails from his garden and took them to show the children in his pre-school. Together they took the snails to the wild area at the back of the school to set them free.

Carrie has a totally different intelligence profile. One of her greatest strengths lies in her interpersonal skills. This is possibly partly due to her home environment. She spends a lot of time with her childminder, both after school and during the holidays. Carrie loves the attention of the childminder's two teenage daughters and spends a lot of time following them around. In doing so, she is developing her interpersonal skills. She knows how to take turns in a one-to-one conversation and asks personal questions like, 'Oh, do you like that?' and makes comments such as, 'I bet you want that cake too, don't you?' Carrie is beginning to be able put herself in somebody else's place and imagine what they might be thinking and feeling. Her intrapersonal skills are also a strength. She talks frequently about how she feels and has a strong sense of right and wrong. She will often verbally challenge other children in the nursery if she feels that they have been unfair to her or to somebody else.

Kishan, on the other hand, has a strong bodily-kinesthetic intelligence and is good at activities that demand logical-mathematical thinking. Samantha's weakest intelligence is bodily-kinesthetic, whereas Kishan's weaknesses are the inter- and intrapersonal intelligences. Their teacher realizes this and works with Samantha to encourage her to take part in more outdoor and physical, hands-on activities, and with Kishan to help him to learn to manage the moment of impulse and discuss his feelings before acting upon them.

Activity: Assessing children's multiple intelligences

Use the checklist to make a quick assessment of children's individual profiles of the multiple intelligences. Write the children's names in the left-hand column. Take each child in turn, thinking about his or her particular strengths and weaknesses. Write a letter 'S' in the column or columns that depicts the child's greatest strength – Carrie's key-worker would write 'S' in both the 'Interpersonal' and 'Intrapersonal' columns, but a 'W' in the 'Naturalist' column. When you have finished, you will have a visual picture of the profile of your group. This can be used to plan activities and groupings that will help children to develop across the range of intelligences.

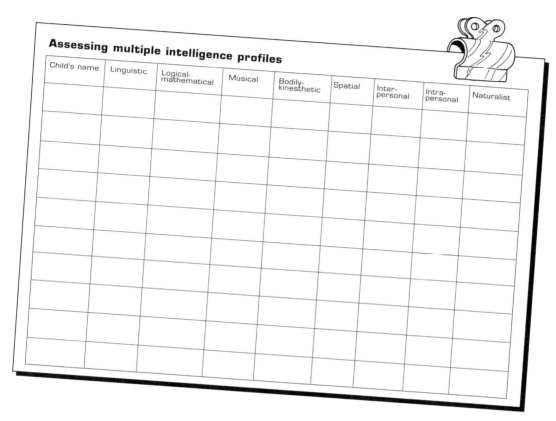

Assessing multiple intelligence profiles

Child's name	Linguistic	Logical-mathematical	Musical	Bodily-kinesthetic	Spatial	Inter-personal	Intra-personal	Naturalist

For full-size photocopiable version, see end of book.

If you want to address the multiple intelligences in a more light-hearted way, you might enjoy considering the children in your care in the light of these intelligence profiles.

A fun way to identify the intelligences of children

Linguistic – The Chatterbox

- Wakes up talking, talks all day, and even talks in his sleep.
- Arrives in the morning with a story about his cat, his dog, his grandma or the dream that he had last night.
- Always has his hand up during story times, plenary sessions and discussion times, and once he starts talking, simply doesn't stop!

Logical-Mathematical – The Lego® Engineer

- Builds amazing models with the Lego® and other construction toys and is often in dispute with other children who want a share of her bricks.

- Is always the first to appear when the computer goes wrong, diving under the desk to try to reconnect the wires before an adult arrives.

- At tidy-up time, organizes toys in an orderly fashion and gets frustrated with other children who don't follow her systems.

Musical – The Singer

- Is always seeking an audience to whom he sings interesting and endless versions of nursery rhymes.

- Can be located at any time within the setting by listening for the sound of singing or humming.

- 'Conducts' music with his hands in assemblies and music or story sessions, and often puts on tapes of music so that he can pretend to conduct a symphony.

Bodily-Kinesthetic – The Gymnast

- Is rarely seen indoors. Can be found at the top of the climbing apparatus, trying to attach a rope to a nearby tree to make a swing.

- Always manages to be first in the line to get to PE sessions.

- Regularly suggests a Brain Gym® session, in which she participates enthusiastically and noisily.

Spatial – The Sculptor

- Works with every conceivable tool and piece of material in the technology area to build models that are too big and elaborate to fit on any shelf.

- Is always covered in paint, glue and clay, no matter how well you tie her apron.

- Can use up the entire stock of paper, cardboard, junk and glue in one short session.

Interpersonal – The Best Friend

● Is often found in the home corner organizing the other children. If they won't be organized, she bosses the dolls around instead.

● Enthusiastically tells you everybody else's business, including the staff's, the children's, her parents' and her neighbours'.

● Can be relied upon to know the ins and outs of every disagreement or squabble that occurs in the setting, whether or not she was in the vicinity.

Intrapersonal – The Sage

● Answers your questions after a lengthy pause, usually by asking you another question.

● At plenary sessions, tells you at length about how he feels about everything that happened to him that morning.

● When you are really busy, tries to engage you in a detailed conversation about a previous conversation that you can hardly remember.

Naturalist – The Bug Hunter

● Brings boxes or jars to school regularly containing insects or worms, which she then wants to release and 'share' during story time.

● Spends hours watching the creatures in the wormery, or the caterpillar or ant farm and has to be reminded constantly to put the lid back on.

● Can be counted upon to persuade her mother to take the guinea pigs home for the holidays.

References

1 Christchurch Health and Development Study, Christchurch School of Medicine, New Zealand, *Pediatrics*, 101, e-page, 1998; www.pediatrics.org

2 Pollitt, E., 'Iron Deficiency and Cognitive Function', *Annual Review of Nutrition*, 113: 521–537, 1993

3 Study by Harlene Hayne et al., University of Otago, New Zealand, reported in *Psychological Science*, May 2002

4 Gardner, Howard, *Frames of Mind – The Theory of Multiple Intelligences*, Basic Books, New York, 1983

5 Maslow, Abraham, *Towards a Psychology of Being*. © John Wiley & Sons Inc, New Jersey, 1998. Reprinted by permission of John Wiley & Sons, Inc.

6 The National School Fruit Scheme; details at www.doh.gov.uk/schoolfruitscheme

7 Goleman, Daniel, *Emotional Intelligence: Why It Can Matter More than IQ*, Bloomsbury Publishing, 1995

8 Song used with kind permission of Mindy Dirks of BACAP Pre-school Groups, Los Gatos, California

9 Reprinted from *Research on Motivation in Education, 3: Goals and Cognitins*, 1989, pp. 73–105, Lepper, M.R. et al., 'Intrinsic Motivation in the Classroom', Extract only, Academic Press, 1989, with permission from Elsevier.

10 Department for Education and Skills, The Standards Site, www.standards.dfes.gov.uk

11 Greenman, Jim, *Caring Spaces, Learning Places: Children's Environments That Work*, Exchange Press, Redmond, Washington, 1988

12 Further ideas can be found on the National Deaf Children's Society's website, www.ndcs.org.uk

13 Kotulak, Ronald, 'Inside the Brain', *Revolutionary Discoveries of how the Mind Works*, Andrews McMeel Publishing, Kansas City, 1997

14 Bruce, Tina, *Learning through Play, Babies, Toddlers and the Foundation Years*, Hodder Stoughton, London, 2001, © 2001 Tina Bruce, reprinted by permission of Hodder Arnold.

15 Young, Susan and Glover, Joanne, *Music in the Early Years*, Falmer Press, London, 1998

16 Wright, J.C. et al., 'Young children's perceptions of television reality', quoted in Healy, Jane M., *Failure to Connect – How Computers Affect our Children's Minds, for Better and Worse*, Simon & Schuster, New York, 1998

17 'Youngsters Unaware TV Ads are Sales Pitch', Reuters Health, 16 April 2002, (article at www. story.news.yahoo.com)

18 From "Guidelines for Young Children Using Computers." Reprinted with permission of Simon & Sheester from *Failure to Connect: How Computers Affect Our Children's Minds – for Better and Worse* by Jane M. Healy, PhD Copyright © 1998 by Jane M. Healy.

19 The High/Scope Educational Research Foundation, www.highscope.org

Appendices

Some principles for planning

- Planning should be a team exercise involving all individuals who work in the setting.

- Plans should be shared with parents and carers.

- Detailed plans for the day should be shared with all adults who work in the setting.

- Children should have the opportunity to contribute to plans through helping to write the To Do list.

- What is planned should be connected to what has gone on before.

- What is planned should be connected to what is likely to happen next.

- Plans should be linked to group and individual targets.

- Plans should be clear enough for an outsider such as a supply teacher to follow.

- Planning should link in clearly to assessment and record keeping, and should identify opportunities for observation and assessment.

- Plans should be flexible enough to allow for a response to the developing needs and interests of the children.

- Consideration should be given to meeting physiological needs when planning.

- Plans should be made for involving children in everyday routines in addition to activities planned by adults and those that children initiate themselves.

- Consideration should be given to addressing the needs of a wide range of groups and ensuring equal access and opportunity.

- Plans for indoor and outdoor areas should be linked so that the outdoors becomes an extension of the indoor environment.

- A balance should be found in planning for both structured and unstructured activity.

- Children should be told of the plans for the day or the session when given the Big Picture.

- Consideration should be given to aspects of brain-based learning such as VAK, the multiple intelligences, use of music, brain breaks and mind mapping.

- Plans should encompass the emotional and social needs of children along with the cognitive, for example, the promotion of self-esteem and emotional intelligence.

Key vocabulary

Brain-based learning: a term used to describe how to apply theories about the brain: to help children to learn more effectively

Brain-based learning circle: a structure to use for the more formal learning sessions Give the Big Picture – assess the starting point – deliver the session in chunks through VAK – build in brain breaks – check for understanding and acknowledge achievements – review the session

Brain break: a short, physical activity to break up a session and refocus and activate the children

Brain Gym®: a brain break activity that involves controlled, cross-lateral movements to connect right and left hemispheres of the brain

Brain stem: the 'primitive brain' which is responsible mainly for survival systems

Cerebral cortex: the largest part of the brain where most high-level thinking processes take place

Decibel clock: a clockface that indicates various noise-levels. The practitioner turns the hand to point to the required noise-level for that session

Emotional intelligence: Daniel Goleman's five aspects of emotional intelligence: self-awareness – management of emotions – self-motivation – handling relationships – empathy

Good listening and good sitting: a system for explicitly helping children to develop good attentional skills

page 87

Good questioning strategies: observe carefully – embed processing cues – ask open-ended questions – allow processing time – listen attentively – reflect back – summarize

Limbic system: the 'mid-brain', which is responsible for some basic functions, such as managing our emotions and some aspects of memory

Maslow's hierarchy of needs: the basic physical needs that must be met if learning is to take place: hydration – nutrition – sleep – movement – attentional systems

Metacognition: having an understanding of the way that you personally learn

Mind mapping: a method of creating a diagram, rather like a flow chart, that allows the brain to work freely and creatively, while making links between concepts

Multiple intelligences: linguistic – logical-mathematical – musical – bodily-kinesthetic – spatial – interpersonal – intrapersonal – naturalist

Neuron: a brain cell

Pole-bridging: talking aloud as you work, describing what you are doing as you actually do it

POSITIVE feedback is: Personal – Objective – Specific – Informative – Timely – Inspiring – Varied – Enthusiastic

SMART targets are: Specific – Measurable – Achievable – Realistic – Time bonded

page 48

Synapse: the connection made between the axon of one brain cell to the dendrite of another

The Big Picture: the overview of the content of the forthcoming session

The Three A's: a motivational system using Acknowledgement, Approval and Affirmation

To Do list: a list developed by the children with an adult at the end of a session, a day or a week, describing what activities and learning they next wish to undertake

Traffic Light: a system for checking understanding – red for 'I don't understand yet', amber for 'I'm not sure' and green for 'I understand'
page 82

VAK: Visual, Auditory and Kinesthetic learning, or 'seeing, hearing and doing'

Recommended reading

Five books about music and learning

1. *The Mozart Effect – Tapping the Power of Music to Heal the Body, Strengthen the Mind, and Unlock the Creative Spirit*, Don Campbell, HarperCollins Publishers Inc, New York, 1997
2. *The Mozart Effect for Children – Awakening Your Child's Mind, Health and Creativity with Music*, Don Campbell, HarperCollins Publishers Inc, New York, 2000
3. *Music in the Early Years*, Susan Young and Joanne Glover, Falmer Press, London, 1998
4. *Music Materials for Early Years*, Leicestershire Music Publications, at www.LMPi.co.uk
5. *Three Singing Pigs*, Kay Umansky, A&C Black, London, 1994

Five books about the brain and learning

1. *Inside the Brain – Revolutionary Discoveries of How the Mind Works*, Ronald Kotulak, Andrews McMeel Publishing, Kansas City, 1997
2. *Endangered Minds – Why Children Don't Think – and What We Can Do About It*, Jane M. Healy, PhD, Touchstone Books, Simon & Schuster, New York, 1990
3. *What's Going on in There? How the brain and mind develop in the first five years of life*, Lise Eliot, Bantam Books, New York, 1999
4. *Start Smart – Building Brain Power in the Early Years*, Pam Schiller, Gryphon House, Inc, Beltsville, Maryland, 1999
5. *Teaching with the Brain in Mind*, Eric Jensen, Atlantic Books, London, 1998

Five books about movement and learning

1. *Smart Moves – Why Learning is not all in your Head*, Carla Hannaford, Great Ocean Publishers, Arlington, Virginia, 1995
2. *Brain Gym*, Paul E. Dennison and Gail E. Dennison, Edu-Kinesthetics, Ventura, California, 1989
3. *The Learning Gym – Fun-to-do Activities for Success at School*, Erich Ballinger, Edu-Kinesthetics, Ventura, California, 1992
4. *Rhythms of Learning*, Chris Brewer and Don Campbell, Zephyr, Tucson, Arizona, 1991
5. *Hopping Home Backwards: Body Intelligence and Movement Play*, Penny Greenland, Jabadao, Leeds, 2000

Five books about play

1. *Outdoor Play in the Early Years,* Helen Bilton, David Fulton Publishers, London, 1998
2. *Learning through Play, Babies, Toddlers and the Foundation Years*, Tina Bruce, Hodder and Stoughton, London, 2001
3. *Supporting Creativity and Imagination in the Early Years*, Bernadette Duffy, Oxford University Press, Oxford, 1998
4. *Educating Young Children*, Mary Hohmann and David P Weikart, High/Scope Educational Research Foundation, Michigan, 2002
5. *Child Care and Early Learning – Good Practice to Support Young Children and Their Families*, Jennie Lindon, Thomson, London, 2003

Five books about intelligence

1. *Emotional Intelligence – Why It Can Matter More than IQ*, Daniel Goleman, Bloomsbury Publishing, London, 1995
2. *Frames of Mind – The Theory of Multiple Intelligences*, Howard Gardner, Basic Books, New York, 1983
3. *Intelligence Reframed – Multiple Intelligences for the 21st Century*, Howard Gardner, Basic Books, New York, 1999

4. *Children's Minds*, Margaret Donaldson, HarperCollins, New York, 1986
5. *The Unschooled Mind – How Children Think and How Schools Should Teach*, Howard Gardner, Basic Books, New York, 1993

Five books about infant and child development

1. *Building Healthy Minds – The Six Experiences that Create Intelligence and Emotional Growth in Babies and Young Children*, Stanley Greenspan, Perseus Publishing, Cambridge, Massachusetts, 1999
2. *The Baby Book*, William Sears, MD and Martha Sears, RN, Little, Brown and Company, New York, 1993
3. *The Secret of Happy Children*, Steve Biddulph, HarperCollins, London, 1998
4. *The Social Toddler – Promoting Positive Behaviour, Understanding Toddlers and Why They Do The Things They Do*, Helen and Clive Dorman, The Children's Project, Richmond, London, 2002
5. *From Birth to Starting School*, Dr Richard Woolfson, Caring Books, Glasgow, 1998

Five books about self-esteem and motivation

1. *Punished by Rewards – The Trouble with Gold Stars, Incentive Plans, A's, Praise and Other Bribes*, Alfie Kohn, Houghton Mifflin Company, New York, 1993
2. *What Young Children Need to Succeed – Working Together to Build Assets from Birth to Age 11*, Jolene Roehlkepartain and Nancy Leffert, PhD, Free Spirit Publishing, Minneapolis, 2000
3. *How to Talk so Kids can Learn – At Home and in School*, Adele Faber and Elaine Mazlish, Simon & Schuster, New York, 1996
4. *Listening to Young Children, The Mosaic Approach*, Alison Clark and Peter Moss, National Children's Bureau, London, 2001
5. *Bringing Reggio Emilia Home*, Louise Boyd Cadwell, Teachers College Press, New York, 1997

Five books about circle time

1. *Quality Circle Time in the Primary Classroom*, Jenny Mosley, Learning Development Aids, Cambridge, 1996
2. *Circle Time*, Hannah Mortimer, Scholastic, New York, 1998
3. *Here We Go Round – Quality Circle Time for 3 to 5 year olds*, Jenny Mosley and Helen Sonnet, Learning Development Aids, Cambridge 2002
4. *Ring of Confidence*, Penny Vine and Teresa Todd, Learning Development Aids, Cambridge, 2002
5. *Time to Talk*, Alison Schroeder, Learning Development Aids, Cambridge, 2000

Some useful websites

www.acceleratedlearning.co.uk
Nicola Call's website. This website gives more information about brain-based learning and information about books, Inset training programmes and brain-based learning resources. There is also a link for contacting Nicola directly.

www.featherstone.uk.com
Sally Featherstone's website. Details here of the wide range of early years materials available from Featherstone Education, including those written by Sally. You can e-mail Sally at: sally@featherstone.uk.com

www.candoclub.co.uk
Nicola Call's website for the 'can do' Club, a new series of children's books with teacher resources for the development of emotional intelligence.

www.alite.co.uk
Alistair Smith's website. Alistair, co-author with Nicola Call of *The ALPS Approach*, is one of the UK's leading trainers and experts in brain-based learning.

www.foundation-stage.info
A website with up-to-date information about the foundation stage, and a discussion board where practitioners can share information and ideas.

www.ndcs.org.uk
The website for the National Deaf Children's Society. A useful website for information about teaching children with hearing disabilities.

www.braingym.com
The official Brain Gym® website.

www.standards.dfes.gov.uk
The DfES Standards Site. Useful website to surf for information such as studies on the National Literacy Strategy and case studies about partnerships with parents.

www.brainresearch.com
An extensive website with in-depth information on all aspects of brain research.

www.thebrainstore.com
The website of a publisher of professional development resources that link neuroscience findings to practical teaching strategies. The site also contains useful links to other resources, such as Eric Jensen's monthly newsletter.

www.ericeece.org
The website for Educational Resources Information Center. Contains lots of useful information about educational research.

www.mindinst.org
The Music Intelligence Neural Development (M.I.N.D.) Institute's home page, containing information about research on the benefits of music education and neural development.

www.naturalchild.org
The website for The Natural Child Project, whose motto is 'All children behave as well as they are treated'. Interesting articles about child development and the respectful care of young children.

www.dana.org
The website for the Dana Foundation and the Dana Alliance, an organization of scientists dedicated to advancing education about brain research.

www.dana.org/kids
'Brainy kid' resources and information for those who work with children using brain-based learning.

www.jlcbrain.com
Eric Jensen's website containing information about training, publications and subscription to a monthly newsletter.

www.circle-time.co.uk
The website for Jenny Mosley's 'Quality Circle Time', containing answers to frequently asked questions about circle time, some free resources and online bookshop.

www.luckyduck.co.uk
A publisher of support materials for teachers who believe in positive approaches to behaviour, such as fostering emotional intelligence and using circle time to develop self-esteem.

www.education-quest.com
The website for Questions Publishing, a publisher of magazines, books and classroom resources. Contains some interesting articles on various aspects of brain-based learning and early years education.

www.m4t.org
The Music for Teachers website where you will find useful information on planning for music sessions and lists of recorded music.

www.highscope.org
The official website for the High/Scope Educational Research Foundation.

Photocopiable material

The following pages contain photocopiable templates of charts and illustrations shown in the book which you may find useful in your early years setting.

The five aspects of emotional literacy

 Self-awareness

 Management of emotions

 Self-motivation

 Handling relationships

 Empathy

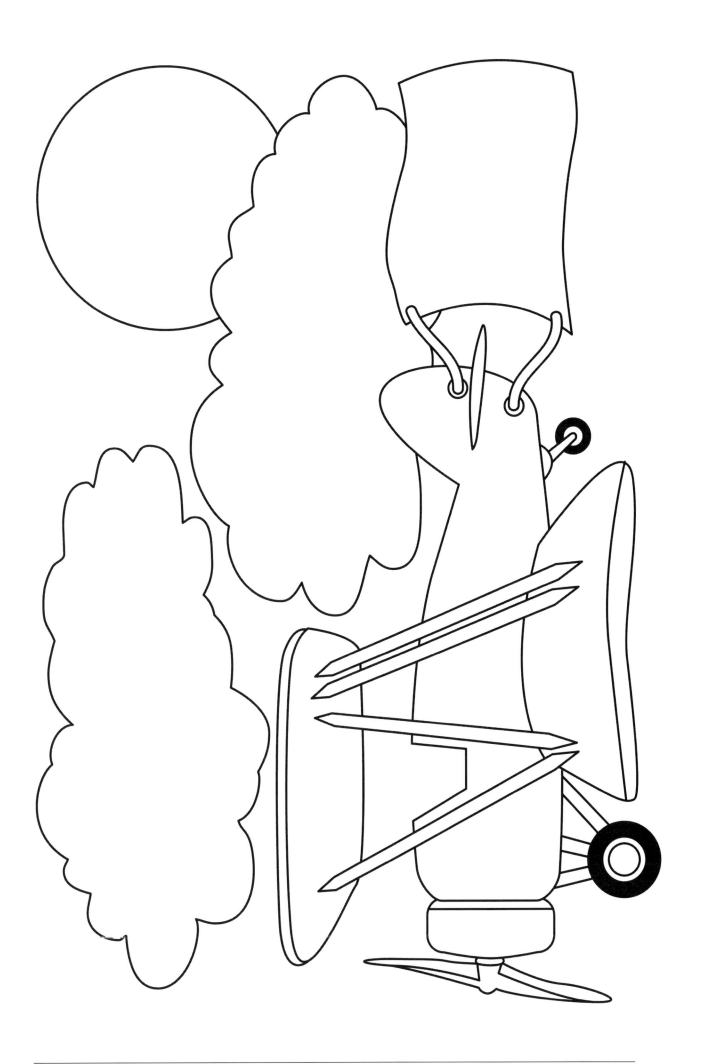

Questions for your volunteer visitor:

Was your initial telephone call dealt with efficiently and in a friendly manner?	
Was the building easy to find?	
How easy would access be for somebody with a disability?	
Were street directions in literature accurate and easy to follow?	
Was the entrance welcoming?	
How long did it take for an adult to approach you?	
How welcoming was the first interaction with staff?	
Were you asked to wear a badge or other identification?	
Were you asked to sign the visitors' book?	
Was there somewhere comfortable to wait?	
Was documentation available in a range of community languages?	
Were signs or notices written clearly and in positive language?	
Were signs and notices written in community languages in addition to English?	
Did you find any documentation or literature about the setting useful?	
Did it seem consistent with the impression from the visit?	
Was adequate information given about children's activities or the curriculum?	
Did the environment seem tidy and orderly?	
Did the children seem confident and relaxed about meeting you?	
Was it clear that the setting encouraged the involvement of parents?	
Did the staff seem confident and relaxed about the visit?	
Did people smile?	
Was there a parents' notice board to look at?	
Was the information on the notice board up to date?	
Was the setting welcoming to both adults and children?	
Were you welcomed and included in the activities?	

The brain-based learning circle

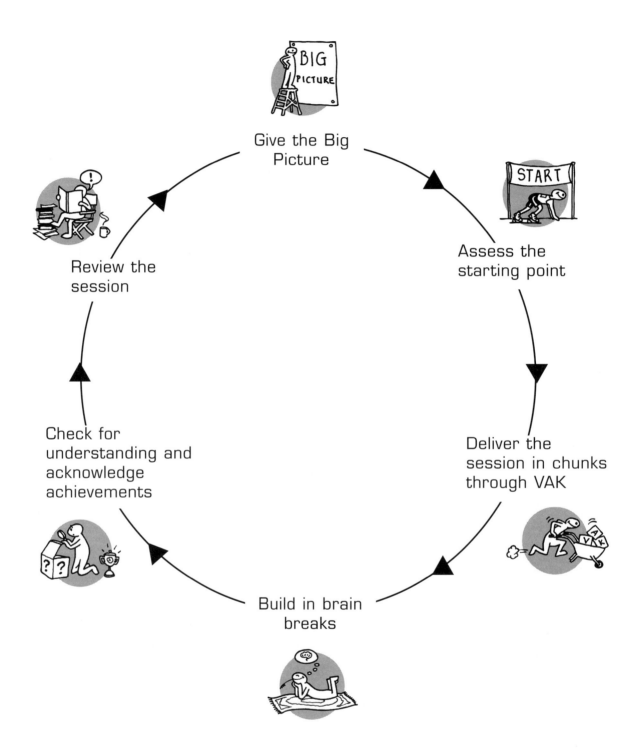

Give the Big Picture

Assess the starting point

Deliver the session in chunks through VAK

Build in brain breaks

Check for understanding and acknowledge achievements

Review the session

Observation sheet: The four-to-one rule

Child's name	Positive	Negative	Neutral	Notes

Forty positive adjectives to use with children:

active	gentle
affectionate	graceful
artistic	healthy
assertive	helpful
calm	imaginative
careful	intelligent
caring	kind
clever	lively
confident	loving
considerate	mathematical
creative	musical
curious	outgoing
determined	peaceful
energetic	persuasive
entertaining	polite
enthusiastic	quick
expressive	scientific
friendly	strong
funny	thoughtful
generous	warm

Positive thinking

Child's name	Positive adjective 1	Positive adjective 2	Positive adjective 3
1			
2			
3			
4			
5			
6			
7			
8			
9			
10			

Observation sheet: Monitoring group-work

Single gender pairs	Mixed gender pairs	Friendship pairs	Single gender groups	Mixed gender groups	Older child with younger child	Single aged groups	Mixed aged groups	Teacher selected groups	Peer selected groups	Other:

Assessing multiple intelligence profiles

Child's name	Linguistic	Logical-mathematical	Musical	Bodily-kinesthetic	Spatial	Inter-personal	Intra-personal	Naturalist

Index

shared environment 59, 98
equipment
 circle time 53
 creative teaching 121
 display 36, 54, 59
 music 53, 112
 play 100, 113

fact vs fiction 111
fantasy 39
feedback 75–7, 143
 four-to-one rule 77–9, 148ff
 useful phrases 82
flexibility 20
four-to-one rule 38, 77–9, 148ff

gardening 16, 51
group-work
 importance of 123
 mind mapping 88
 monitoring 124, 148ff
 organizing groups 126
 Plan – Work – Recall 127
 practical jobs for children 125
 social skills 123

hearing deficit 63
hierarchy of needs 13, 142
home corner 100, 112
home–school partnerships 43–4
hydration 13–14

impulsive behaviour 22, 26
independent learning
 attention skills 62–70
 concentration 71–5
 environment 51–2, 55–6
 language 75–84
 play 95
instructions, giving 64–5, 71–2
intelligence, teaching for
 creative teaching 117–22
 emotional intelligence 21–7
 group-work 122–7
 multiple intelligences 135–9
 teaching through VAK 127–34
interactions with children 38–9
interpersonal intelligence 139
intrapersonal intelligence 139
IQ 10

key vocabulary 142–3
kinesthetic learning 71, 106, 133–4, 138

language 10
 comments 78, 81
 feedback 75–7, 82
 four-to-one rule 38, 77–9, 148ff
 in the home 75–6

importance of 83
pole-bridging 83–4
positive adjectives 78–9, 80, 148ff
positive thinking 79–80, 148ff
positive vocabulary 76, 77–9, 80–1
processing time 71–2
questioning 82, 122
learning styles 71–2, 106
 see also VAK
linguistic intelligence 137
lining up strategies 68–70
listening skills
 good listening 62, 64, 142
 good sitting 62, 63, 71, 128, 142
 music 102, 103
 processing time 71–2
 turn-taking 63
literacy sessions 73
logical-mathematical intelligence 138

management of emotions 21, 22–4, 26, 27,
 63–4, 94
memory 10
mind mapping 85–7, 142
 applications 87
 assessing knowledge and understanding 88
 challenging and extending learning 90–1
 group-work 88
 making connections 89
 reasons for 92
 revisiting previous learning 90
 sharing ideas 88
motivation 21, 25, 39, 145
movement 18–19
 brain break activities 107–9
 physiological need for 106
multiple intelligences 135, 142
 assessing 137–9, 148ff
 balance in teaching 136
 bodily-kinesthetic 138
 interpersonal 139
 intrapersonal 139
 linguistic 137
 logical-mathematical 138
 musical 138
 naturalist 139
 spatial 138
 see also VAK
music 15, 18, 19
 choosing 102
 classical music 102, 103, 105
 equipment 53, 112
 film music 103
 listening skills 102, 103
 'Mozart Effect' 102
 opportunities 103
 other cultures 103
 pop music 103
 preparation 101

using 101, 102–3, 104
variety 101, 103, 105
musical intelligence 138

National School Fruit Scheme 16
naturalist intelligence 139
neurons 9, 143
noise levels 67–8
numeracy sessions 73, 113
nursery class 11–12, 18, 51
nutrition 10, 15–16

pair work 111
parents and carers 43
   communication 44, 111
   home–school partnerships 43–4
   involving parents 46–7
   welcoming systems 45, 148ff
   workshops 45
passive behaviour 22
photocopiable material 148ff
physical needs 13
   attentional systems 20
   hydration 13–14
   movement 18–19
   nutrition 10, 15–16
   sleep 17–18
Plan – Work – Recall 127
planning 100, 141
play
   12 important features 96
   balance 93, 99
   home corner 100, 112
   independence 95
   indoors and outdoors 99
   making sense of experience 95, 100
   management of emotions 94
   planning 100
   practising behaviours 96
   practising new skills 95
   principles 100
   purpose 93, 94–6
   real-life items 100, 113
   sensitive intervention 93–4, 97
   in shared accommodation 98
pole-bridging 36, 83–4, 143
positive language 38, 76, 77–9, 80–1
   adjectives 78–9, 80, 148ff
   comments 76, 81
   four-to-one rule 38, 77–9, 148ff
   self-talk 37
   thinking 79–80, 148ff
practical jobs for children 125
pre-school 11
puppets 27, 36, 53

questions
   for confidence 35
   for productive dialogue 82
   strategies 142
   'What would happen if?' 122
quiet areas 18

relationships 21, 22–3, 24, 25, 77
relaxation 18

self-awareness 21
self-belief 35, 37
self-control 22
self-esteem 28–30, 31, 76, 145
self-motivation 21, 25
self-talk 37
shared spaces 59, 98
sharing 95
sitting, good 62, 63, 71, 128, 142
sleep 17–18
social skills 24, 25, 35, 77, 95, 123
spatial intelligence 138
speaking skills 24
special needs 29
speech therapy 63
staff morale 76
staying on task *see* concentration
synapses 9, 143

technology
   computers 110, 111, 114–15
   skills 110, 111
   television 111
   variety 110–11, 112–13
television 111
temper tantrums 63–4, 71–2
The Three A's 26, 27, 38, 39–42, 143
   Acknowledgement 39, 41, 67
   Affirmation 39, 42, 71
   Approval 39, 41
thinking, positive 79–80, 148ff
timing 73, 74
To Do lists 35, 53, 143
'Traffic Light' system 53, 143
turn-taking 63

understanding 88, 95, 100

VAK (visual, auditory and kinesthetic learning)
   20, 127–8, 143
   auditory learning 131–2
   balance in teaching 127
   kinesthetic learning 71, 106, 133–4, 138
   visual learning 129–30
visual learning 129–30